AIRMANSHIP

Carey Edwards

THIRD EDITION

FOREWORD BY

CAPTAIN ERIC 'WINKLE' BROWN
CBE DSC AFC MA RN

BLACKER LIMITED

I would like to dedicate this book to the late John Garnons-Williams who thought I might be of some use, introduced me to the helicopter world and rekindled my interest in flying for the RAF.

He was a true gentleman and an excellent instructor.

Carey Edwards
First published in 2008
Second edition published 2013

This revised and updated third edition published 2017
by Blacker Limited
Text copyright © Carey Edwards 2017

British Library Cataloguing in Publication Data
A catalogue record for this book is available from the British Library
ISBN 978-1-897739-12-9

Picture Credits
Every effort has been made to identify and seek permission from photographers to use photographs included in the book.
Many thanks to those who have given permission.
Cover photograph from Markus Wisler

Contents

Abbreviations

AAIB	Air Accidents Investigation Branch	ICAO	International Civil Aviation Organisation
ACARS	Aircraft Communication & Reporting System	IFE	In-Flight Entertainment
		ILS	Instrument Landing System
AMSL	Above Mean Sea Level	INS	Inertial Navigation System
AoA	Angle of Attack	IRS/U	Inertial Reference Sys/Unit
APU	Auxiliary Power Unit	JFK	New York International Airport
ASR	Air Safety Report	KLM	Dutch National Airline
ASI	Air Speed Indicator	LOFT	Line Oriented Flying raining
ATC	Air Traffic Control	LMQ	LMQ Limited
ATIS	Automatic Terminal Information System	LPC	Licence Proficiency Check
		MCDU	Multi-fn Control Display Unit
CA	Captain	NM	Nautical Mile
CB	Cumulo Nimbus	NDB	Non-Directional Beacon
CFIT	Controlled Flight Into Terrain	OAT	Outside Air Temperature
CRJ	Canadair Regional Jet	OPC	Operators Proficiency Check
CRM	Crew Resource Management	PIA	Pakistan International Airlines
CVR	Cockpit Voice recorder	PFD	Primary Flight Display
DME	Distance Measuring Equipment	PF	Pilot Flying
		PNF	Pilot Not Flying
ECAM	Electronic Centralised Aircraft Monitor	QRH	Quick Reference Handbook
		RAF	Royal Air Force
EICAS	Engine Indicating and Crew Alert System	RVR	Runway Visual Range
		SBS	Special Boat Service
EPR	Engine Pressure Ratio	SOP	Standard Operating Procedures
FDR	Flight Data Recorder		
FE	Flight Engineer	TO	Take-off
FL	Flight Level	TOGA	Take-off Go-Around
FMC	Flight Management Computer	TWR	Tower
FMS	Flight Management System	V1	Take-off decision speed
FO	First Officer	V2	Initial climb-out speed
FOD	Foreign Object Debris/Damage	VR	Rotation speed
FTL	Flight Time Limitations	VMC	Visual Meteorological Conditions
GPS	Global Positioning System		
GPWS	Ground Proximity Warning System	VOR	VHF Omni-directional Radio

Foreword

··

My first reaction on seeing the title and size of this book was to ask myself how anyone could find so much to write on such an abstract subject. Well, if you are of a similar view then you are in for a surprise. Most pilots could give their thoughts of airmanship in a couple of lines, but Carey Edwards opens up a whole new world of in-depth study on the subject, and it is nothing if not thought provoking. If you have a know-it-all approach to aviation, this book will shake you to the core; if you want to learn all about aviation then read deeply of this content and you will have helped yourself along the path of knowledge.

To some aviators airmanship is a mystery, and if you like mystery stories you will know that some avid readers cannot resist looking at the last chapter to find the solution before starting on the content. If you do this with Carey's book, you can be sure you'll be anxious to read the content if you want to be a professional and a survivor.

Captain Eric 'Winkle' Brown CBE DSC AFC MA RN
FORMER CHIEF NAVAL TEST PILOT

Prologue

···

It is late autumn 1684 in the Eastern Atlantic. An armed merchantman, the George, is almost becalmed but on the last sector of what has been an extended trip.

'Second mate, I notice the sheets are loose and you have eased the main halyards; pray tell me your reasoning, young man.'

'Well Cap'n, in lighter winds I understand the sails should be fuller to gain the maximum power from their shape.'

'That would normally be the rule, but below 5kt it is often preferable to tighten the sailcloth, so that the centre of pressure moves aft and the sail flattens off. Otherwise, the air flow coming around the leading edge is not sufficient to complete its journey around the leeward side and the sail will stall. What were they teaching you at ground school eh? This is a good opportunity for you to advance your art and experiment for yourself, but don't put the crew under too much stress, as we are all a little fatigued and there might be a heavy workload up ahead for us.'

'Aye, aye Sir.'

'And try to resist calling me Sir – it is not appropriate.'

'Aye, aye Cap'n'

A few hours later, standing on the fore deck, the captain had watched the development of cirrus and medium level clouds from the northwest, as well as the steady dropping of the mercury. The ship's navigator was summoned.

'Mr Trestock, we are in for a front and judging by the rate of change in the pressure I think it will be severe. The wind has already veered and strengthened considerably and we are still a long way off its passing. How do you see it?'

'I agree, and these October fronts will often have embedded CBs in them.'

'That's very true. Recheck the waypoints you have plotted, particularly the last leg into the Irish Sea as we will have a major crosswind drift, and don't forget the variance or we will be on the Fastnet rocks for sure. Finally, take a sighting as soon as you can, as we will lose the sun presently and much will depend on an accurate latest position.'

'Will do.'

'Purser, I have a hunch things may not go as smoothly as we would like so will you assemble all hands by the rear galley as I wish to brief them?'

The captain arrived and quietly addressed the assembled seamen.

'OK lads we are now well past 30 West and in the final stages of this sector. We are entering a high-risk area for there are many privateers on the prowl. The weather will deteriorate and it will be a bumpy ride. Ensure the passengers are secure and cargo made fast, and if you hear, see or feel anything you don't like, I want you to let me know instantly. Even though you may think it is absurd and unnecessary, it might be vital information pertinent to the safety of this ship. Right, now close all hatches and cross check.'

'Quartermaster, I need a report on the water state and our endurance, and let me know when we are down to 50 gallons, because we may need to divert into Shannon.'

Back on deck the captain spoke to the first mate. 'Mr Stables, let's check the configuration'.

'what do you think?'

'Well you're the captain, but in view of the impending weather, I would be inclined to set the fore staysails, the foresail, the main and main top gallant, both double reefed, and leave the mizzens at standby.'

'I agree. Go through the configuration change checklist with the bosun, and have the sails set accordingly.'

As the day wore on, the storm well and truly began to take hold and the swell increased markedly. Waves began crashing over the bow and pouring along the deck, which was not a safe place to be. Recognising the threat and the likelihood of the crew making errors in these conditions, the captain ordered non-essential crew down below.

'Ship ahoy off the port quarter at 4 leagues! It is a brigantine bearing 265 and tracking east nor'east.'

'Set heading 110 degrees,' called the captain and, to the first mate, 'Briefing for you, bosun, nav, the gunnery officer and a couple of the experienced hands in my cabin on the hour. Pass the word.'

'Gentlemen, do I have your attention? Good. As you can see we are being stalked by this privateer and it is clear his intent. The threat is real and I intend to manage it effectively. I am sure they will track us closely through the night until the weather has eased, because even they would not stomach a fight in these conditions – but actually that may be our best chance of survival. The options are to run, surrender or fight it out – what are your thoughts?'

'Well, we can't outrun them and we all know what happened to the Celia when she surrendered.'

'I concur. I think the weather is our friend. I suggest we appear to flee but, as they close, to reverse course, come up under their stern and engage them. Hopefully, we will cause sufficient damage to affect our escape under cover of darkness. All agreed?'

'Aye'.

'Timing will be critical, and I would like us all to maintain good situation awareness and think ahead; much will depend on this. Guns, prepare the crews and run through the drills – we will not know until the last moment from which side we will engage. Nevertheless, I want you to fire at your discretion for maximum damage. What are your orders?'

'To prepare and drill both port and starboard battery crews, and when required to fire at my discretion for maximum damage.'

'Correct – good luck. Now, brief your teams accordingly – there is not a moment to lose.' The George's only defence was to try to disable the attacker by damaging its helm with a close barrage of fire as the George passed beneath its stern. This was a tricky manoeuvre but had to be done in the circumstances: they had no chance against a well-armed ship in a standard encounter.

As dusk began to fall, the brigantine had closed significantly and was now tracking the merchantman, the wind was howling and the ships were losing sight of each other temporarily in the swell and the rain squalls. Several rolls of thunder with the inevitable flash could be heard in the distance.

'The wind is gusting 30kt, shall we take in the top main gallant Cap'n?'

The sails were pulling hard under the load but the captain needed the speed for manoeuvre. There was a 1500lb strain limitation on the mainsheet block but the sails would probably tear before then. It was a balanced risk and not an easy decision.

'No, abide with me a while, I need the extra power with the wind shearing as it is, but we'll keep an eye on it nevertheless.

'Right helmsman, now is the moment! Bring her up to the wind and keep her as full and by as you can, and bosun set the wind angle monitor.' The wind angle monitor was the captain's own invention, a device that gave out a sharp whistle when the ship was sailing almost head to wind, with little angle of attack and in danger of an inadvertent tack.

The ship turned rapidly onto a northerly course and began heeling alarmingly. As expected, the predator reacted and was now positioned upwind and abeam to port.

'Helm, come up more under their lee, point as high as you can but watch bank angle – if you begin losing rudder control, shout and we will free the sheets a bit and unfurl the flying jib to add lift to the bow.'

The ship was already taking water over its lee gunwale as the overpowered sails forced it over by nearly 35 degrees to the vertical, and as the bow dipped into the towering waves the rudder would clear the water. The captain had always thought the rudder too small and not equal to the task, but it would have to do.

The George was now within close separation of the brigantine, who could not understand why they were undertaking such manoeuvres in those violent seas. They just maintained a comfortable position as they did not wish to be so close hauled – it really was an undesirable point of sail for the conditions. The strain in the rigging and the shrouds of the George was audible, the hull juddered in the troughs, and the timber from masts and yards creaked and groaned.

'Cap'n I am worried we may be too fast and are getting high on our approach.'

'I think with this head wind we should just manage it but we'll monitor it carefully. However, let's add some drag, so backwind the main staysail.'

Unfortunately, though, a few minutes later there was a sudden break in the squall.

'Cap'n we are too fast, the wind has backed and we will overshoot. Go-around!'

'Helm, come about – hard a port! Bosun, sheet in the main sail as hard as you can, we need full power. Good call, Mr Stables, I was fixated on their position and hadn't noticed the wind change.'

The sails flapped violently and the ship hurled itself onto the opposite tack; men were hauling sheets and halyards under the direction of the bosun on the fo'c'sle. Fortunately, however, the privateer had reacted badly to the wind change and had swung to port, losing its leeway. This left them in an ideal spot to be attacked and the captain pressed home the advantage.

'Come up as high as you can and close on their stern. Message to guns: it will be a starboard side barrage – read back!'

'Starboard side barrage for the guns.'

Suddenly a loud whistle was heard. 'Helm, port 5 and hold it steady,' said the captain calmly reacting to the monitor.

The roar of a dozen guns crackled over the wind, just as the George had rolled on the top of a wave. This meant the full force of the barrage was directed downwards through the helm and stern of the brigantine, ripping spars and splintering timber in its path.

'Bear away, heading 120. It will be dark soon and by the time they have sorted that lot out we will be away. A brilliant shot guns, break out some rum for the crew.'

A few days later they were on their final approach nicely lined up on the centre line into the Mersey channel, and from there safely landed their passengers, crew and cargo at Liverpool docks. On the quarterdeck the captain, bosun and the second mate reflected on the journey.

The bosun remarked, 'Well, that was an eventful trip – but we came through,' and, turning to the young man, added, 'Stick with this captain, lad, and you will learn all you need to know about seamanship.'

The captain smiled.

'That's kind of you to say bosun, but sadly to the contrary – although I am an experienced captain I still have a lot to learn,' she replied, and thought of the stories and advice her grandfather and great seaman had given her, particularly about the exploits and professionalism of the Venetian masters and Roman galleon captains.

Introduction

· ·

Airmanship. It is nothing new folks (except the 'air' bit), but let's not be picky – the principles of airmanship have been around for centuries. They have been more or less understood, but this book aims to make them more specific and to offer some suggestions as to how they might be learned.

I suppose the reason I felt the need for such a book stems from my own experience. During my early flying training career there was a lot of talk about the importance of airmanship, but I didn't really know what it meant. I certainly knew I didn't have any, because that was what I was regularly told. A typical debrief would be thus:

'Edwards, not a bad trip, of course not great by any stretch of the imagination – and your airmanship is poor.'

To this I would hesitantly reply, 'Can you tell me what you mean?' which instantly cast me as someone unable to accept criticism and a troublemaker to boot.

'Yes, your lookout is non-existent.' From then on I imitated one of those nodding toy dogs you see in the back of cars. To no avail, the Edwards airmanship score continued to hover just above dire.

'Your checks were not done properly.' The checks became a source of pride, with not a comma omitted.

'You are rough on the controls.' The purchase of silk inner gloves would surely alleviate this problem.

I sought sanctuary in the venerable books that the Air Force produced.

A pamphlet on airmanship would certainly have the answer. It was about circuits and signal squares with a bit on downwind checks, and of course lookout – but of no use at all.

Fortunately, in the nick of time and after scraping through my basic course I was transferred to helicopters, where clearly the reasoning employed by the Air Force was that an uncoordinated, illogical and irrational pilot without any airmanship would be best suited to an uncoordinated, illogical and irrational flying machine, where any employment of airmanship would only add to the confusion. In fact, they probably hoped the two might very well cancel each other out and something of use could be the result.

Thankfully, this was not far from the truth. My years of flying helicopters finally taught me a little about airmanship, entirely of course from watching others and taking copious mental notes, some of which I have managed to remember and which I will try to share with you here.

Quotes from the old and bold

In my quest for an understanding of airmanship I sought out several very experienced and respected pilots and asked them the same question: what is your definition of airmanship?

These are some of their replies:

- Not getting caught out.
- Being professional.
- Common sense.
- Inner know-how.
- Being in control of the situation.
- The stuff that keeps you out of trouble. Experience – there is no substitute for it.

And the most common response was:
- I know what it is but I just can't put it into words.

Airmanship defined

OK then – what is it?	Well, it is those intangible things a pilot has to operate an aircraft safely.
What about the job?	OK, it is what a pilot has to get passengers to their destination on time, or to complete a rescue mission – safely.
Anything else?	Well, I suppose pilots with good airmanship also do the job efficiently, so do not waste fuel and other resources.

So what do they use to do all this?	Easy. Knowledge of the aircraft, principles of flight, met, navigation and anything else that is relevant to the job.
Is that all, just know-how?	Alright, they also need some flying, navigation and planning skills, and so on.
What about their approach to their work, their attitude?	Most important! Airmanship is about being professional, disciplined and conscientious.
What about the way they interact with other people?	You're persistent aren't you!
Yes. We've been waiting nearly 100 years to know what it is.	I suppose it is good airmanship to look after your team, co-operate with other people, have integrity and all the other good stuff.
So, is airmanship then the knowledge, skills and attitudes a pilot employs to operate an aircraft effectively, efficiently and safely?	Yes – that's it! That's airmanship in a nutshell.
In that case, what are the knowledge, skills and attitudes – and how can I improve them?	Now that would be useful to know.....

Attempting to define it and giving pilots some ideas on how they can improve their own airmanship – is really the purpose of this book.

Airmanship: The (technical, operational and non-technical) knowledge, skills and attitudes aircrew employ to operate an aircraft effectively, efficiently and safely.

The book

I believe that airmanship is a combination of good technical, operational and non-technical knowledge, skills and attitudes. These are things such as knowledge about the aircraft and its operation, the ability to fly the aircraft smoothly and accurately, self-discipline and the ability to manage the task and the people around you. The result is that the job is done well and safely.

I have therefore organised the book along these lines. It is not completely neat and tidy, but is hopefully a workable framework, and I ask readers to go with the flow. Inevitably there will be overlaps and duplication, but I am not too worried about this because in the flight deck, cabin, tower, ramp or hangar they all come together in the job anyway.

You will notice that there is a lot more on the non-technical subjects than the technical and operational, but this does not reflect any proportional level of importance – they are all equally important. It is just that similar processes apply to the technical and operational subjects, and illustrating airmanship principles in these areas is relatively straightforward.

The non-technical subjects, however, tend to be more complicated, are open to challenge and require different approaches. Furthermore, most pilots have a lot of information and exposure to technical and operational things, rather than to the non-technical subjects shown in this book. Finally, this is not meant to be an academic document, nor is it proposing to be definitive; but hopefully it is something that will help aviators be safer, more effective and efficient.

I have concentrated on airmanship as seen from the cockpit, because that is what I know, and I would not presume to suggest that there is an automatic read across to other professions; nor indeed to imply that other disciplines are not part of the airmanship domain.

However, if there are similarities, then I will leave it to those professionals to translate the useful bits to their own operations, and make their own relevant connections.

Getting it right

Inevitably, as pilots tend to think of the term airmanship in the context of avoiding accidents, I will explore many of those throughout the book, but I would like to begin on a positive note and highlight a few examples from many, where the airmanship of the crew resulted in an extraordinary feat.

Sioux City

On the 19th July 1989 a United Airlines DC-10 was flying from Denver to Chicago at 37,000ft when the No.2 engine (mounted in the tail) suffered an uncontained engine failure that severed the lines of all three hydraulic systems and so caused a total hydraulics failure. This meant that the crew, as well as losing an engine, had lost all their flying controls.

The aircraft, which was in a descending turn to the right at the time, failed to respond to inputs from the autopilot, which was promptly disconnected, but then also to manual control. The captain, Al Haynes, realised what was happening and leveled the aircraft by bringing back the No.1 power lever, although the aircraft continued its descent. Fortunately an off-duty training captain, Dennis Fitch, was on board and he offered his help to the crew, which was gratefully accepted. Captain Fitch took control of the power levers from behind the central console, and the crew took their time discussing the problem and experimenting with the control they had available, eventually manoeuvring the DC-10 to line up with the south-westerly runway at Sioux City. They managed to lower the gear successfully and to control the phugoid movements of the aircraft as best they could.

To make matters worse, the ailerons were stuck in a position that made left turns impossible to control, but the crew managed to make a high-

A United Airlines DC-10 (Frank Duarte)

DC-10 cockpit showing the throttle quadrant that Captain Fitch had to operate. (Serge Bailleul)

speed flapless landing on the airfield. Unfortunately, a roll developed at the last moment that they had no time to correct, and the starboard side struck the ground heavily, causing the aircraft to cartwheel, turn on its back and burst into flames. Nevertheless, an astonishing 185 passengers and crew survived the accident.

Having a strong understanding of principles of flight, systems and engine performance meant that the crew had the confidence and belief to control the aircraft sufficiently to enable it to arrive at an operational airfield in a fairly level attitude. Furthermore, the way the crew interacted with each other, with the cabin crew and with external agencies was exemplary, and meant they used all the resources available to them. This extraordinary feat of airmanship resulted in the survival of the majority of those on board.

QF32

On the 4th November 2010, a Qantas Airbus A380 Flight QF32 departed from Singapore for Sydney. At around 7,000ft in the climb the No.2 engine exploded, which caused massive damage to the aircraft with the loss or degradation of almost every aircraft system including hydraulics and electrics.

The crew were faced with multiple warnings and were given the impression that they only had one fully functioning engine. However, remaining calm and professional, the five flightcrew (Captain Richard de Crespigny, First Officer Matt Hicks, Captains Dave Evans and Harry Wubben, and Second Officer Mark Johnson) together with the Cabin Service Manager Michael Von Reth, meticulously went through the checklists associated with the 60 odd ECAM messages, identified what had happened and communicated with the passengers. One of the two hydraulic systems was losing all its fluid, 2 of the electrical buses had failed, and the APU wouldn't take up any load, so the aircraft went into essential power mode. There were also pneumatic leaks causing air conditioning and cooling system failures, and the fuel jettison system didn't work. During this one and half hours, whilst they worked through pages of the checklists and sub checklists, they were required to make several decisions, such as discounting the checklist item to transfer fuel, even though they had both lateral and longitudinal fuel imbal-

A Qantas A380 (Qantas)

ances due to the fuel leak, with possible C of G issues. They also needed to almost manually calculate the landing distance required and approach speeds, as the flight management system would not accept the multiple failures, so they worked around the problem only to discover they needed 3900m to stop – the runway back at Singapore had 4000m.

Finally after carrying out a handling check and extending the gear by gravity, they made a high-speed overweight landing with 35% roll capability, reduced flaps, spoilers and braking functions. Even with speed and stall warnings, Captain Richard De Crespigny touched down at the exact point at the right speed – and stopped within the 100m they had left to spare. However they then made an exceptional and correct decision not to evacuate, as they felt the passengers were safer inside in a controlled environment, as they had fuel pouring out of the left wing, the No.1 engine could not be shut down and the brakes reached over 950°C. Their crew performance, communications, leadership, teamwork, workload management, situation awareness, problem solving and decision making resulted in no injuries or significant mental trauma to the 450 passengers and crew. QF32 will remain as one of the finest examples of airmanship in the history of aviation.

The exploded No 2 engine of QF32

CASE STUDY

British Airways B777 G-YMMM at Heathrow following the crash landing

British Airways 777 at London Heathrow

On the 17th January 2008 a British Airways Boeing 777 G-YMMM was on short finals to land at Heathrow when it suffered a double engine failure caused by ice build up in the fuel system. The failure was not immediately obvious as it was not connected to typical warnings that trigger actions. Nevertheless, Captain Peter Burkill, in the 30 seconds he had before impact, made the decision to allow the co-pilot to continue flying which freed up his thinking capacity, started the APU, transmitted a Mayday call and tried to analyse the fault. He recognized the speed was decaying due to too much drag and reduced the flap setting, which prevented the aircraft hitting the ILS aerials, which would probably have caused a fire and possible loss of life. An outstanding display of airmanship and captaincy.

CASE STUDY

Bristow G-TIGK

On the 19th January 1995 a Super Puma G-TIGK operated by Bristow helicopters was approaching a North Sea oil platform in typical rough winter weather for that region. Whilst descending through 3,000ft the aircraft was struck by lightning which caused severe vibration. The crew transmitted an emergency call, briefed the passengers of a possible ditching and diverted to the nearest platform. A few minutes later the tail rotor failed, a catastrophic emergency for helicopter pilots. Nevertheless, the crew, Cedric Roberts and Lionel Cole reacted swiftly, by shutting down both engines, entering autorotation, briefing the passengers, and transmitting a further Mayday call. After arming the flotation gear at the exact moment, they executed a perfect engine off landing in heavy seas, which meant that the aircraft remained afloat. This enabled all crew and passengers to board a liferaft from which they were rescued.

Bristow Helicopters Super Puma G-TIGK afloat in the North Sea

In addition to these and others mentioned later in this book, the Atlantic Southeast Airlines Embraer engine failure, the Air Transat A330 fuel loss and the Northwest Airlines DC10 cargo door failure are also incidents showing great examples of airmanship.

Technical Elements

Introduction

Although airmanship is sometimes thought of as an intangible thing surrounding the job of flying, I think it is more fundamental than that and is very much a central part of the job. Having sound technical knowledge, skills and attitudes is a prerequisite to good airmanship. If you don't know your aircraft and how it works, or if you struggle to fly and navigate accurately, then I can't see how you can demonstrate a great deal of airmanship.

Technical knowledge

In 1899 Charles Duell, Director of the US Patent Office, apparently said on suggesting the closure of the office, 'Everything that can be invented has been invented', which is a great story because it is perfectly understandable. I often think the same thing today, even though I am constantly amazed at the never-ending innovations and clever devices that people develop.

The reason I quote this story is that we can never really know everything, or be sure we know what will happen in the future. Aviation has countless examples of people being caught out because the aircraft or systems did not work as advertised.

And why is this?

The answer is simple: it is because they have been designed, built and maintained by human beings who are not only capable of making errors, but cannot possibly anticipate all the conditions and circumstances that will arise in the future.

Who would expect that reverse thrust would deploy in the cruise (Lauda Air), or that a type of wiring covering would cause a catastrophic fire (Swissair), or that an engine failure would cause complete loss of hydraulics (Sioux City), or that disabling a temperature probe would also disable the take-off configuration warning (Spanair).

The Virgin Atlantic Airbus A340 – Heathrow 1997

A brilliant example of the importance of knowledge was the Virgin Atlantic Airbus A340 incident in 1997, which occurred when the aircraft carried out an emergency landing on Runway 27L at Heathrow with the left main landing gear only partially extended. The landing gear had been jammed by a wheel brake torque rod, which had disconnected from its brake pack assembly and had become trapped in the keel beam structure. The associated torque rod pin was subsequently found beyond the end of the runway at the departure airport.

While preparing to land the commander reviewed the 'Landing with abnormal landing gear' procedure in the QRH, which called for the crew to shut down all engines prior to touchdown. Realising that this would deprive them of all electrical and hydraulic power and thus control, the commander elected to amend the QRH procedure by shutting down No.1 and 4 engines prior to touchdown followed by the No.2 engine on his command, and to delay shutting down the remaining engine until into the landing roll. This was an extraordinary action in the heat of an emergency, when strict adherence to the emergency checklist is drummed into modern pilots from the start of their training, but it resulted in far less damage to the aircraft than would otherwise have been the case, and the subsequent amendment of the QRH.

The Virgin Atlantic A340 landing at Heathrow 1997 (Perry Harris)

Good airmanship, therefore, is knowing as much as you can about your aircraft and what it does, because it will be this information that will help you when all else fails. Much more importantly, it releases precious capacity in stressful situations as your are not diverting mental energy trying to work out what is happening. It is also about fully understanding the principles of flight so that you can use clues that may be absent from other instrumentation, and ensure that when operating modern fly-by-wire aircraft, you are still flying the aircraft rather than the aircraft flying you. There have been a number of accidents and incidents in recent years where automation has been a significant factor. Over-reliance on automatic controls and systems management has inevitably led to pilots monitoring less, losing situation awareness and having less understanding of how the aircraft works. Modern aircraft are flown almost entirely using a flight management system and autopilot, so it is critical that pilots are completely familiar with how the automatics work, their limitations, quirks and capabilities.

Airmanship is also about knowing your aircraft performance and weight and balance, so that if you notice all passengers have been loaded at the back then it might not be wise to apply power too abruptly. It is about understanding weather, ensuring you are not complacent and have a healthy respect for the laws of nature. Finally, it is about being completely up to date with navigation theory and systems, both in the air and on the ground. Not understanding the limitations of GPS or flight envelope protections is going to catch out a lot of people in the next twenty years.

Birgenair

On the 6th February 1996 Flight ALW 301, a Boeing 757, departed Puerto Plata for a charter flight to Frankfurt near midnight. At 80kt during the take-off the captain found out that his ASI wasn't working properly although the co-pilot's indicator seemed to be indicating correctly. While climbing through 4700ft the captain's ASI read 350kt (the actual speed was about 220kt); this resulted in autopilot increasing pitch and reducing power reduction in order to lower the airspeed. At that time the crew got 'Rudder ratio' and 'Mach airspeed' advisory warnings. Both pilots appeared to become confused when the co-pilot stated that his ASI read 200kt decreasing while getting an excessive speed warning, followed by a

CASE STUDY

stick shaker warning. This led the pilots to believe that both ASIs were unreliable. Finally realising that they were losing speed and altitude they disconnected the autopilot (which, fed by the captain's faulty ASI, had reduced the speed close to the stall speed) and applied full thrust. Following an aural GPWS warning the aircraft struck the ocean 8 seconds later. The incorrect ASI readings were possibly caused by an obstructed pitot tube, which had been left uncovered for 3–4 days prior to this flight.

Probable cause: The crew's failure to recognise the activation of the stick shaker as a warning of imminent entrance to the stall, and the failure of the crew to execute the procedures for recovery from the onset of loss of control.

CASE STUDY

Adam Air

On the 1st January 2007 a Boeing 737 of Indonesian airline Adam Air took off from Surabaya for Sulawesi. During the cruise and following problems with the Autopilot, the crew were engaged in resolving an Inertial Reference System (IRS) malfunction, but lost control of the aircraft with the loss of 102 lives. The report suggested that the crew had insufficient knowledge of the IRS system and also failed to monitor the aircraft state, a good example of the validity of the first rule in emergencies – 'Fly the aircraft'.

An Adam Air B737

Air Asia

On 28 December 2014 an Air Asia Airbus 320 on route from Surabaya to Singapore at 32,000ft had a Rudder Travel Limiter failure, caused by cracking of a solder joint. The crew performed the ECAM actions but kept getting repeated warnings. After the fourth warning it appears that the Captain, who had over 20,000 hours including military aircraft and nearly 5000 on type, left his seat and pulled the FAC (Flight Augmentation Computer) CBs, a procedure he had observed engineers carry out on the ground. However, this caused the autopilot and autothrust to disconnect leading to an upset and subsequent fatal stall, from which the flightcrew were not able to recover and the loss of 162 lives.

How is this learned?

There is no substitute for hitting the books and getting stuck into the theory, but it is also important to notice the theory working in practice and to fully understand how things work. This does not mean experimenting when you have a couple of hundred passengers on board, normally preceded by a 'I wonder what will happen if we pull this circuit breaker', or seeing if your aircraft can reach 41,000ft, which tragically occurred in a corporate jet accident where the crew were not trained in high level flight. But it does mean reading up on the systems and then observing what actually happens in flight, and of course, keeping up to date with changes in procedures, techniques and legislation.

However, this needs to be supported by an organisational culture that promotes continuous learning and encourages those who want to learn more. It is also important that training staff challenge crews on their knowledge on a regular basis. But this should be done not with the intention to catch them out, but to maintain a high level of expertise and professionalism.

Helios

On the 14th August 2005 a Helios Boeing 737 departed Larnaca in Cyprus for Prague, via Athens. Prior to departure the aircraft had undergone a pressurisation check, which required manual control of the outflow valves. These valves remained in the manual position, which meant that the aircraft did not automatically pressurise in the climb, so as the cabin altitude passed 14,000ft the Cabin Altitude aural warning sounded in the cockpit. The crew wrongly identified this as a Take-Off Configuration warning – which had the same sound – and contacted their engineering centre to establish what the fault was. They also had an Equipment Cooling System warning, which was consistent with the fans being starved of oxygen. However, they were overcome by hypoxia before they could establish the real cause of the warning and the aircraft climbed to FL340 on its pre-programmed route with the autopilot engaged. It then took up the KEA VOR holding pattern outside Athens, and remained there for two hours prior to running out of fuel and crashing.

The Helios B737 in the hills near Athens. (Kostas Iatou)

Technical skills

Together with sound technical knowledge, good airmanship requires skill levels to be as high as they can be. Of course there are natural pilots, but the rest of us need to develop our skills so that they are as good as they can be, and that just means we have to put more effort and application into achieving this standard. Being able to fly accurately and smoothly, and also to have the skills to handle emergency situations, is a key part of good airmanship.

American Airlines A300B

On the 12th November 2001 an American Airlines Airbus A300 took off from New York and encountered wake turbulence in the climb out. The co-pilot who was flying the aircraft reacted with excessive and unnecessary use of the rudder that was beyond the design limits of the aircraft, which resulted in the entire vertical fin separating and causing the aircraft to crash in the suburbs.

CASE STUDY

Crash site of American Airlines A300B (Michael Wilusz)

Asiana Boeing 777

On 6 July 2013 a Boeing 777-200ER operating as Asiana Airlines flight 214 was on approach to runway 28L when it struck a seawall at San Francisco International Airport resulting in the deaths of 3 passengers and the complete loss of the aircraft.

The flight was vectored for a visual approach to runway 28L and intercepted the final approach course about 14 nautical miles (nm) from the threshold at an altitude slightly above the desired 3° glidepath. This set the flight crew up for a straight-in visual approach; however, after the flight crew accepted an air traffic control instruction to maintain 180 knots to 5nm from the runway, the flight crew mismanaged the airplane's descent, which resulted in the airplane being well above the desired 3° glidepath when it reached the 5nm point. The flight crew's difficulty in managing the airplane's descent continued as the approach continued. In an attempt to increase the airplane's descent rate and capture the desired glidepath, the pilot flying (PF) selected an autopilot (A/P) mode (flight level change speed [FLCH SPD]) that instead resulted in the autoflight system initiating a climb because the airplane was below the selected altitude. The PF disconnected the A/P and moved the thrust levers to idle, which caused the autothrottle (A/T) to change to the HOLD mode, a mode in which the A/T

Asiana 777 at San Francisco

does not control airspeed. The PF then pitched the airplane down and increased the descent rate. Neither the PF, the pilot monitoring (PM), nor the observer noted the change in A/T mode to HOLD.

As the airplane reached 500ft above airport elevation, the point at which Asiana's procedures dictated that the approach must be stabilized, the precision approach path indicator (PAPI) would have shown the flight crew that the airplane was slightly above the desired glidepath. Also, the airspeed, which had been decreasing rapidly, had just reached the proper approach speed of 137 knots. However, the thrust levers were still at idle, and the descent rate was about 1,200ft per minute, well above the descent rate of about 700 fpm needed to maintain the desired glidepath; these were two indications that the approach was not stabilized. Based on these two indications, the flight crew should have determined that the approach was unstabilized and initiated a go-around, but they did not do so. As the approach continued, it became increasingly unstabilized as the airplane descended below the desired glidepath; the PAPI displayed three and then four red lights, indicating the continuing descent below the glidepath. The decreasing trend in airspeed continued, and about 200ft, the flight crew became aware of the low airspeed and low path conditions but did not initiate a go-around until the airplane was below 100ft, at which point the airplane did not have the performance capability to accomplish a go-around. The flight crew's insufficient monitoring of airspeed indications during the approach resulted from expectancy, increased workload, fatigue, and automation reliance.

One of the most fascinating things in life is watching experts doing very difficult things but making them look easy. If you carefully observe a juggler with five balls, changing pace and trajectory, talking at the same time and throwing the odd ball back and forth to a colleague, you really cannot see what special thing they are doing that enables them to achieve such a standard. They just seem to be slowly throwing a ball up, followed by another and another and then catching them, again nice and slowly, and so on. Well, I can do that – what's the big deal! Except that I can only juggle a couple of balls for a very short period of time, and with a lot of erratic and hasty hand waving and grimacing. Asking me at the same time to spell my name would be well beyond my available mental capacity.

The same occurs when I am watching an experienced and capable pilot fly an ILS in a crosswind and turbulence. The airspeed indicator does not move in the slightest, and the localiser and glide slope indicators remain fixed in the central position, but that's clearly because they have become stuck. Fortunately for the pilot also, the turbulence and wind miraculously disappear for the duration of their approach, and they are able to arrive at the precise touchdown point at the correct speed, for a smooth landing.

Piece of cake, let me have a go. Some success. I have practised several go-arounds; I have ensured all controls have full and free movement; I have explored the flight envelope (and will be sending a report to the manufacturer's flight test department, in case they have missed something); and I have played a tune on the throttles that a cello player would be proud of. But then during my approach the instruments were playing up, and the wind and turbulence were so much stronger and more erratic...

The frustrating thing is that we know what to do – we just can't do it. However, over time we slowly start developing these skills, but then the better we get the more we appreciate how difficult it is, and the number of levels that are still above us.

As well as QF32 and the other previously mentioned examples, the Java, Gimli and Hudson River incidents are superb examples of brilliant skill levels and would always be considered as demonstrating great airmanship, so it is worth reminding ourselves of what happened.

CASE STUDY

Java

In 1982 a British Airways Boeing 747 G-BDXH was cruising at 37,000ft between Kuala Lumpur and Perth on a clear night when it inadvertently flew through a cloud of volcanic ash. All four engines flamed-out and several of the flight instruments were erratic. Captain Eric Moody, without the benefit of hindsight, did not say, 'Not to worry chaps, we have just flown though some ash, so we will drift down to a lower altitude in some cleaner air, relight the engines and continue on our way – tell the purser he can carry on with our dinners, I'm actually rather famished.' No. They had little idea what had happened, they were on standby electrics, there were sparks flying at the windscreen and it all smelt a bit smoky. Nevertheless, they went through the drills calmly and professionally and tried to determine what had gone wrong, while carrying out a 180° turn to divert to the nearest suitable airfield, Jakarta.

As they glided down they could not restart the engines after several attempts, and as the cabin altitude climbed Captain Moody decided to increase the rate of descent to get to a lower altitude, as the First Officer was having difficulties with his oxygen supply and Captain Moody felt he needed the First Officer more than precious height. To add to their problems they could not be seen on Jakarta radar, nor could they receive any VOR or DME information, and even the INS was unreliable. Finally, at 13,000ft they managed to restart all four engines in turn – though they were then forced to shut one down again – and they continued their approach to Jakarta. On finals Captain Moody was faced with little visibility through the damaged windscreen and the landing lights were ineffective, but even so he was able to make a successful landing.

The expertise in managing the emergency by both the flight crew and cabin crew (who by their outstanding actions were able to keep passengers less traumatised), and finally the skill in safely landing a 747 on three engines through an opaque windscreen at night was airmanship at its highest level.

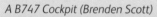

A B747 Cockpit (Brenden Scott)

The Gimli Glider

On the 23rd July 1983 an Air Canada Boeing 767 flying from Montreal to Ottawa ran out of fuel at 35,000ft, mainly due to technical refuelling problems and an error in calculation. Without power to generate electricity, all the electronic gauges in the cockpit became blank, leaving only standby instruments, consisting of a magnetic compass, an artificial horizon, an airspeed indicator and an altimeter. Unable to reach a suitable airfield, the crew elected to land at Gimli, an unused ex-military airfield in the vicinity, that the co-pilot remembered from his military days. They had no flaps or slats and the nose gear failed to lock down. The captain, Bob Person was, however, a glider pilot and used all his gliding skills, including side slipping the large aircraft until quite close to the ground, to successfully land without any injuries to those on board or on the ground. The 767 touched down on runway 32L within 800ft of the threshold. The nose contacted the runway and the Boeing came to rest short of a drag racing strip. Now I am not suggesting that we all go out and learn how to glide, but it is an example of how a particular skill came in handy when the seemingly impossible occurred.

The Air Canada B767 after gliding into Gimli

The Hudson River

On the 15th January 2009 US Airways Flight 1549, an Airbus A320 took off from runway 04 at La Guardia New York en route to Charlotte, North Carolina. The first officer was pilot flying but as they were reaching an altitude of 3,000ft the crew saw a formation of Canada geese. Before they knew it, the windscreen turned dark brown and several loud thuds were heard. Both engines began to lose power and there was a burning smell. Captain Chesley Sullenberger took over control of the flight and informed ATC about their emergency situation: 'This is Cactus 1549, we lost thrust in both engines and are turning back toward La Guardia.' It quickly became evident that they were not able to reach La Guardia. A possible landing at the Teteboro Airport was considered, but the captain decided that they would not be able to land safely on the short runway in the middle of a built-up area, so he told ATC 'We're going to be in the Hudson.' The aircraft then ditched into the freezing river and all occupants evacuated the airplane, climbing onto the wing and entering escape slides. The captain ensured that everyone had left the aircraft before leaving himself, which illustrates that airmanship does not stop until the flight has been safely completed. The most impressive part of this emergency was making the decision quickly that a ditching was inevitable. In these situations there is a strong feeling that it can't be happening, and this sense of denial can cause people to clutch at straws and do nothing rather than taking action, which in this case meant getting on with making a successful landing on the water.

The A320 after ditching in the Hudson River. (Janice Krums)

How is this learned?

Good training is essential to the development of the right skills. This does not just mean the amount, but the quality as well. To ensure someone learns a skill, start with the basics and build up to the required standard in a logical, thought-out process. This is the key to good training. An instructor who is able to instantly recognise faults and, more importantly, the cause of those faults, will develop a student's skills in the right direction so that bad habits aren't formed. Furthermore, people need to be able to learn one particular skill properly and sustainably before moving onto another one. It is a bit like spinning plates, if one skill starts being lost then it needs to be brought back up to speed before introducing a new one. It is often said that there are mainly 2 ways to learn something, either by shock or repetition.

Once trained, however, the only way to maintain one's skills is practice, practice and more practice. Varying the environment, resources and objectives are the best ways in which people can continuously develop their skills, whenever possible throwing in unusual emergencies and situations, so that a wide range of experiences are recorded in that powerful thing – the subconscious. Getting hands-on as much as possible until activities become motor programmes (things that we do without much thought), which then releases capacity for managing other things. Drill, drill, drill. This is why there is no substitute for experience, because experience allows us to do many more things naturally, so that we can concentrate on the key problem. When they find themselves in tricky situations, inexperienced people are just trying to spin far too many plates.

Obviously, simulators and other synthetic devices are wonderful tools for skill development, but running through emergencies in a quiet cockpit on the ground, or even mentally thinking through how you would handle a situation are also valuable techniques for honing those skills. After all, because of automation, modern flying is 95% a mental activity, as there is now very little that requires just a basic manual skill. In fact until someone really gets their head around what they are trying to do, then they struggle to execute the action. Ask any golfer learning to get out of a bunker. Even raw data manual instrument flying requires an intense level of concentration rather than pure flying skill. So if you can practise visualising what you would do in varying situations, then when something does happen you have an established thought-process and mental picture to refer to, and you are not trying to make several decisions at the same time.

Technical attitudes

Airmanship is the protective shield, when all else fails. Those who have it in abundance try to understand as much as they can about their aircraft and its systems, because deep down they know that one day this knowledge might be critical. But I am not just referring to aircraft systems – these are only a small part of the knowledge base. Principles of flight, the environment, meteorology, navigation systems and air traffic systems are also major subjects of which pilots need to have a good understanding.

I am disappointed at the prevailing attitude these days which is, 'You don't need to know all that technical stuff. If it is in the green it's good and if it is in the red it's bad – and the checklist, EICAS or ECAM will tell me what to do.' I know this is acceptable and the policy some manufacturers are adopting during initial or conversion training, who have to consider the lowest common denominator and training costs, but I think better airmanship is developed when pilots go on to learn more about their aircraft. There is a valid argument that too much information can be confusing and distracting (which I can quite easily relate to – I am often confused and distracted without trying). It is also a concern of manufacturers and operators that pilots with a little knowledge might make their own amendments to the recommended procedures and get into trouble. This is a reasonable and understandable concern, and there have been incidents of this occurring. Accident data has shown that when crews interpret and make up their own procedures, they more often than not get it wrong – but I think this only occurs when there is incomplete knowledge.

However, on balance I still think that the more knowledge you have, the better pilot you will be. Understanding the aircraft means you will be expecting what happens, especially at critical times. The last thing a pilot needs in an emergency is to be confused or distracted by something the aircraft is doing that they don't expect or understand. It reduces their capacity and thus their performance.

An example is that on the Airbus 320/330 aircraft, the design engineers have determined that the rudder and aileron displacement required to reduce side-slipping during a single engine failure creates more drag than that caused by the side slipping aircraft. The aircraft computers are therefore designed to calculate the optimum amount of slip so that there is a minimum overall drag; it is a compromise between induced drag, derived from the aerodynamics, and form drag from the structure and shape of the aircraft, as well as preventing spoiler deployment. It is called the beta target and operates under certain configuration and power difference conditions. What this means in the cockpit, however, is that even though the pilot has centred the slip indicator, the aircraft will still be side slipping, and when beta target is operating the side-slip indicator turns blue. A pilot not fully understanding the design principles of beta target might be unnecessarily distracted if he or she is carrying out a single-engine go-around, or spending too much time on the rudder trim and not monitoring height or airspeed. If you are expecting it and know what is happening then it doesn't consume any thought.

Furthermore, some people know that if they don't continually sharpen their skills, then when they need them it all gets a bit fraught. A friend of mine decided to see how long it would take him and his co-pilot to fully put on their oxygen masks in the cruise when surrounded by lunch, charts and other typical paraphernalia. He admitted they were struggling to make it within the prescribed time, and might practise doing it properly a bit more in future!

Those with great airmanship also try to develop their skills to as high a level as they can. As soon as they are able to do something well, they press on to do it even better, or in different conditions.

And of course there is self-discipline, which is about following procedures and checklists even when there doesn't seem to be the need; being careful and monitoring meticulously, but above all being honest about your capabilities and performance – and putting the effort in to improve. It is also about double-checking things when you have the slightest doubt, and taking the trouble not only to plan beforehand but tidy up all the loose ends afterwards.

I was told a disappointing story by a long haul captain recently. He returned early to the flight deck from his bunk having had sufficient sleep, and relieved the cruise first officer. He then reviewed the hourly fuel checks that the first officer had been recording, and noticed that the 'actual' fuel for the next few hours had already been filled in!

One of the biggest challenges of self-discipline is debriefing after a flight. It is very tempting to feel it is all over, nothing happened, so why bother to talk about it – but it is important that you learn and share that learning, no matter how trivial. This then sets a routine that keeps you on your toes. If you know there will be a debrief after every flight where even small indiscretions will be talked about, then it sure encourages you to avoid the big ones.

MD-11 landings at Newark and Narita

On the 31st July 1997, about 01:30 local time, a MD-11 operated by Federal Express crashed and overturned while landing on runway 22R at Newark International Airport. The regularly scheduled cargo flight originated in Singapore the day before with intermediate stops in Penang, Taipei and Anchorage. On board were the captain and first officer, who had taken over the flight in Anchorage for the final leg to Newark, one jump seat passenger and two cabin passengers. All five occupants received minor injuries in the crash and during their escape through a cockpit window. The aircraft was destroyed by impact and a post-crash fire. The National Transportation Safety Board determined that the probable cause of this accident was the captain's over-control of the aeroplane during the landing and his failure to execute a go-around from a de-stabilised flare. Contributing to the accident was the captain's concern with touching down early to ensure adequate stopping distance.

Picture of the FedEx MD-11 at Newark after an eventful landing. (M J Scanlon)

In an almost identical accident on the 23rd March 2009 another Fedex MD11 landed in high winds at Narita airport. The aircraft bounced twice, landed on its nose gear bounced again, whereupon the left wing broke. This caused the aircraft to roll left and catch fire, ending up inverted.

Fedex MD11 at Narita

Operational Elements

Introduction

Airmanship is not just about safety. It is about getting the job done well. Anyone can be just safe and risk-averse, but we would still be living in caves if this was all we did. If you think about it, putting 300 or so people into a metal container barely a centimeter thick, surrounded by fuel and several fires at over 500°C, then accelerating them to 400mph, 8 miles high, in an environment full of others doing the same thing, where there is little oxygen and the temperature is minus 60°C, is a fairly risky activity; and yet pilots achieve this successfully every day.

Airmanship is also about doing the job efficiently and effectively. We do not have an infinite abundance of resources, and those with airmanship know how to use those resources well. One of the key roles of a pilot of commercial airlines is looking after the passengers, the brand and ultimately the company's profitability. Some consider profit to be a dirty word but I think it is essential for airline safety. I won't go so far as to say that profitable airlines are safe airlines, but there is ample evidence to show that unprofitable airlines are potentially unsafe. The temptation to cut corners and reduce safety margins is far too great for an airline barely surviving.

LaMia Avro RJ

On 28 November 2016 a LaMia Avro RJ 146 took off from Santa Cruz in Bolivia at 22.18 with a maximum fuel load of 9,300 kg to Rionegro in Colombia.

During the cruise, the CVR recorded various crew conversations about the fuel state of the aircraft and they could be heard carrying out fuel calculations. At 00:42 one of the pilots could be heard to say that they would divert to Bogota to refuel but at 00:52 a further conversation took place, shortly after the aircraft was transferred to Colombian ATC, with the crew deciding to continue to Rionegro.

CASE STUDY

At 02:45 the aircraft entered the hold at GEMLI and although they requested a fuel priority they completed 2 holds before starting their approach at 02:54 leaving the hold about 12,000ft, whilst waiting for another aircraft beneath them to land. At 02:56 they lost all engines due to fuel starvation and the aircraft crashed 10nm from the runway at 02:58 with the loss of 77 people.

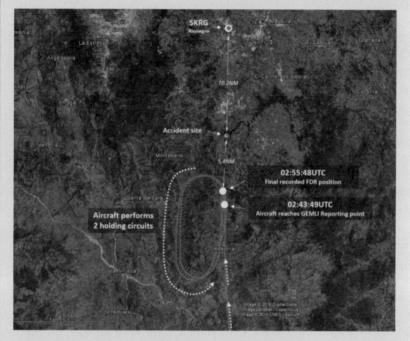

The final track of the LaMia 146 as it ran out of fuel in Colombia

But the above does not just apply to commercial operations. The military, search and rescue units, and Humanitarian Relief Organisations are conscious of the image that they portray and pilots doing silly things occasionally damage their reputations.

The operational aspects of airmanship are about knowing the parameters that you operate in, understanding the rules of the game and being good at playing it.

Operational knowledge

Operational knowledge is about understanding the people, systems and processes that affect the job you are trying to do. Experienced pilots seem to know how the dispatchers operate, what engineers are doing and how to get the best out of air traffic. They anticipate things, do not get fazed when it all goes awry and have the capacity to communicate knowledgeably with the various different agencies, who seem to those less clued-up to be just conspiring to keep the aircraft on the ground.

Pilots with sound airmanship get the job done efficiently, do not waste resources, their time or other people's time, and keep their customers happy. They do this because they know what goes into ensuring an aircraft and its passengers get from one place to another on time. They know how baggage handlers retrieve unaccompanied luggage and how long it takes; they know the security procedures at airports; they fully understand the commercial operations and how the company makes its revenue. They understand the economics of their particular area of aviation – and this includes those in the military, as even the military do not have unlimited resources. And in flight, because they have been monitoring the whereabouts of other traffic, they don't put pressure on busy controllers by asking for a flight level they know they haven't a hope in hell of getting.

How is this learned?

The answer is not rocket science. Find out what other people do and the difficulties they face. Talk to engineers, ramp staff, controllers and anyone else who will affect the operation of your aircraft. Ask questions. Find out what they would prefer you to do as the pilot and what they find hinders their work. Spend some time with them so that you can see first hand the pressures they are under, the environment and information that they work with. It isn't really great airmanship to be sitting in a warm cockpit in shirt sleeves and getting frustrated because the de-icing crew are taking too long, when they are working in a minus 15°C blizzard, soaked through from falling several times on the icy tarmac, and struggling to free frozen valves.

As a bare minimum, occasionally spend time in the tower, at approach control and at the en-route centre so that you can fully understand the great air traffic game. They always welcome pilots and can't understand why they get so few visits, but it is an extremely valuable day out. If you are exceptionally lucky you might be able to have a go in an ATC simulator. Just forgo the

Wednesday morning 'four ball' for once, get down to somewhere like the UK's southern en-route centre at Swanwick, and plug into the controller's station; learn what resources are available to you in an emergency and see the flexibility inherent in the system – a flexibility of course you can exploit! Don't forget, if you don't ask then you don't get, and you can't ask if you don't know what you can ask for.

Operational skills

Operational skills are very much the realm of planning, organising and effectively implementing a plan. It is about good time and task management, and it is about keeping ahead of the situation by knowing what needs to be done and when.

We all know who the good operators are, and also those who seem not to care. My own experience flying helicopters in support of the Army really drove home the differences. A typical day, sometimes non-stop at ultra low level for over 6 hours with rotor-running refuels (accompanied by military supplied 'cordon-bleu' sandwiches), would require punctual multiple pick-ups and drop-offs in 10 mins legs. These would often be to eight figure grid references (+/-10 metres), in almost any weather, maintaining constant radio communications on more than one frequency, and trying to avoid being shot at or flying over a national border, which would result in much diplomatic noise and severe reprimands from the station commander.

There were those of us who invariably turned up late, followed the programme aimlessly, didn't react if the situation changed, and ended up causing considerable problems to those on the ground by taking twice as long to finish the task. This was mainly because we refuelled whenever the light came on, couldn't take full troop loads because we had filled up with too much fuel, or instead just over-torqued the gearbox if it was getting close to tea-time, and were constantly getting lost or dropping the chaps off in the wrong place. Any sign of inclement weather and we promptly packed up for the day, where we might find the odd hole in the fuselage when we returned to base.

The good operators however, thought about the next four or five sectors, planned refuels, suggested changes to the plan to help those on the ground and to make it more efficient, communicated constantly to the troops and to operations, and varied their routing to avoid trouble. They knew what was happening in an ever-changing situation and could plan several steps ahead, while still flying safely and smoothly, so that troops disembarked in a reasonable state. They kept an eye on the weather, knew the limits and flew to them, and always got the task done without putting anyone at risk. They also knew when to say no!

In the commercial world I am sure there are those who play catch-up on a Canarsie approach into JFK when given a late runway change – and invariably forget something. And there are those who have set up most of the possible scenarios, and then briefed and rehearsed them well before top of descent.

Operational Attitudes

The main operational attitudes are being committed to planning, preparation, and making sure the customer's needs are met, including going the extra mile when needed.

I think there are 2 types of people. There are those who are activity focused and those who are results focused. Activity focused people love a mess, so they have lots to do. They don't achieve much, but they look very busy and work long hours, and are motivated by the praise they get for beavering away. Fire-fighting and problem solving are what they are good at, and they even don't mind putting out the same fire over and over again. Doing things is what is important, rather than achieving things, because once something is achieved then there is nothing else to do, which is a nightmare for an activity focused person.

A results focused person on the other hand is only interested in getting results as efficiently and to highest practical standard. They know that to get a result they need to plan and continually think of what can go wrong so that they can avoid the need to put out fires. They are resourceful, use resources properly but do not waste them. They prepare, organise themselves, others and things and use techniques such as checklists, colour coding, and alarms to ensure the plan is on track. They quickly adopt technological devices and get the most out of them to ensure they release capacity to deal with inevitable changes in the plan. In essence it is the old 6 Ps. Prior planning and preparation prevents poor performance.

A final debatable attitude is the willingness to take risks and to accept responsibility for the decision and the consequences. This does not mean at the expense of safety, but there are times when taking a small risk prevents a lot of problems for a lot of people.

How is this learned?

Surprisingly, a lot of operational skill development can be done in a classroom with case studies and dynamic exercises, because again it really is a mental game. Using these techniques, pilots can learn to juggle several things at once, plan, re-plan and re-plan again on the hoof, and get used to continuous double and triple checking, so that nothing is missed in the chaos. They also can learn how to stay calm, relaxed and able to think clearly when the pressure is on; and finally they recognise the importance of good communications.

But there is no substitute, of course, for experiencing the real thing, although there is little opportunity from a training point of view to influence the course of events or go over things again when the task needs to get done. However, what you can always do is debrief the task, to see how things could have been done better and what you will do differently next time. This also highlights the mini tools, processes and techniques that you can develop to add to your armoury for the future. Good operational attitudes are about getting the job done well and ensuring the customer is more than satisfied. This means taking the trouble to understand what is required, to suggest better options and being willing to compromise. It is about going the extra mile and being flexible, but not wasting time and other resources. It is about balancing safety and the job, not being risk-averse, but knowing where the line is and not breaking rules or regulations. And again it is about having the all-important self-discipline, taking the trouble to be prepared, not allowing yourself to make assumptions, and constantly thinking ahead.

ICAO Core Competencies

In 2013, an ICAO working group developing guidance for national authorities to manage the introduction of Evidence-Based Training (EBT) produced a set of core pilot competencies (Appendix 1 of DOC 9995 Manual of Evidence-Based Training). The group agreed 8 competencies of which 3 were considered to be mainly technical and the other 5 non-technical. These competencies are really the fundamental building blocks of airmanship as I am attempting to describe in this book. As part of that working group I was involved in the development of the competencies and their performance indicators, particularly as the non-technical competencies were based on the non-technical performance indicators that were developed by LMQ and described in earlier editions of this book.

The only area that caused much debate was whether knowledge was a stand-alone competency. The very plausible argument for not doing so, was based on a dichotomy that as the definition of a competency was the combination of knowledge, skills and attitude to perform a task to a prescribed standard, it therefore was illogical that knowledge can be a competency. It would be of no surprise to readers that I was strongly of the opinion as explained earlier that I believe knowledge is essential for good airmanship, and therefore argued for knowledge to be upgraded to a competency on its own. I put forward an analogy that an egg can be an ingredient in many recipes but it can also be a meal in itself, but to no avail!

I felt the academic argument above was less important than a situation where knowledge was not recognised as core, as this would frustrate trainers and examiners in future from identifying and fixing the root cause of a pilot's performance. Therefore, as many airline and helicopter operators support this view, I will introduce 9 competencies, as I think they clearly explain airmanship and enable it to be trained, which has not been done formally for many years, and is the main reason for this book.

The ICAO Technical Core Competencies and their Performance Indicators – (Airmanship clearly defined).

Application of Procedures

- Identifies the source of operating instructions.
- Follows SOPs unless a higher degree of safety dictates an appropriate deviation.
- Identifies and follows all operating instructions in a timely manner
- Correctly operates aircraft systems and associated equipment
- Complies with applicable regulations.
- Applies relevant procedural knowledge.

Aircraft Flight Path Management – Automation

- Controls the aircraft using automation with accuracy and smoothness as appropriate to the situation.
- Detects deviations from the desired aircraft trajectory and takes appropriate action.

- Contains the aircraft within the normal flight envelope.
- Manages the flight path to achieve optimum operational performance.
- Maintains the desired flight path during flight using automation whilst managing other tasks and distractions.
- Selects appropriate level and mode of automation in a timely manner considering phase of flight and workload.
- Effectively monitors automation, including engagement and automatic mode transitions.

Aircraft Flight Path Management Manual

- Controls the aircraft manually with accuracy and smoothness as appropriate to the situation.
- Detects deviations from the desired aircraft trajectory and takes appropriate action.
- Contains the aircraft within the normal flight envelope.
- Controls the aircraft safely using only the relationship between aircraft attitude, speed and thrust.
- Manages the flight path to achieve optimum operational performance.
- Maintains the desired flight path during manual flight whilst managing other tasks and distractions.
- Selects appropriate level and mode of flight guidance systems in a timely manner considering phase of flight and workload.
- Effectively monitors flight guidance systems including engagement and automatic mode transitions.

Knowledge Core Competencies (used by some operators).

- Demonstrates practical and applicable knowledge of limitations and systems and their interaction.
- Demonstrates required knowledge of published operating instruction.
- Demonstrates knowledge of the physical environment, the air traffic environment including routings, weather, airports and the operational infrastructure.

- Demonstrates appropriate knowledge of applicable legislation.
- Knows where to source required information.
- Demonstrates a positive interest in acquiring knowledge.
- Is able to apply knowledge effectively.

The DHL Airbus Baghdad

The DHL Airbus A300 was hit by a SAM-14 surface-to-air missile while climbing through 9,000ft shortly after departure from Baghdad. The missile struck the wing, penetrated a fuel tank and ignited the fuel, burning away a large portion of the wing. The aircraft then lost all hydraulics and the crew (Captain Eric Genotte, First Officer Steve Michielsen and Flight Engineer Mario Rafoil) attempted a landing back at Baghdad Airport. The captain remembered learning about the Sioux City incident and used thrust levers to control the roll and pitch of the aircraft. After a missed approach they were forced to circle the field until they finally landed heavily on runway 33L, 16 minutes later. The Airbus veered off the left side of the runway, travelled about 600m through soft sand, struck a wire fence and came to rest on a downslope. This was the first successful landing of a transport aircraft without flying controls, and another great example of superb airmanship and an exceptional use of all the above core competencies.

The DHL Airbus showing the missile damage to the port wing

CASE STUDY

Non-technical Elements

Introduction

The non-technical elements of airmanship are sometimes considered synonymous with the subject of Human Factors, which will be discussed in more detail later, or CRM (Crew Resource Management). CRM is familiar now to most aircrew, and in the early days was ironically often labelled as just another name for airmanship. But this would be incorrect as CRM covers only some of the human factors subjects, and for simplicity could be defined as the non-technical part of airmanship.

Non-technical knowledge

Airmanship requires an understanding of how we function both physiologically and psychologically. This means understanding how the body functions in an aviation environment: the effects of pressure, lack of oxygen, acceleration and stress; how we get disorientated and the causes of disorientation; visual illusions such as white out, mind set, night vision, how things appear different at night, and so on. It is definitely about understanding jet lag, fatigue and circadian rhythms, which are the subject of a later chapter. Knowing how and why people behave, the psychology behind relationships, group dynamics, motivation and personality are also important.

Airmanship includes an understanding of how humans process information, the limits of short and long term memory, response times, motor skills, fixation, tunnel vision and how the brain blocks out sounds under stress. These essential pieces of knowledge will not be covered in this book, but can be found in a range of other excellent publications such as the UK CAA's CAP 737.

Finally, it includes how errors are made and the whole subject of human factors.

Non-technical skills

It is important not just to know how human beings function and how they make mistakes, but also to know how individuals can improve their performance, manage their relationships with others better and avoid error. For this they need to develop key skills to enable them to apply what they have learned into practice. The range of non-technical skills have chapters of their own.

Non-technical attitudes

This is where things tend to merge into one another and overlaps exist between the non-technical, operational and technical attitudes, such as self-discipline that have been mentioned earlier. But it doesn't matter which box they go into at the end of the day. However, if I was going to identify attitudes that I would consider to be purely non- technical, I would highlight the following:

- Having self-respect. In other words, the confidence to do and say things that you believe are right, and ensure that you are treated with respect. Recognising that you can and will make mistakes.
- Having respect for others. Giving others the right to their opinions and to do things that are important to them, including respecting their values, culture and habits. Being tolerant when people make mistakes and taking care of the effect your behaviour has on others.
- Being prepared to learn from experience. Accepting that you do not know it all and probably never will, and taking the trouble to learn things that you need to know.
- Having integrity. Being open and honest with yourself and with others.
- Being positive. Trying to ensure things are successful rather than looking for excuses for failure.

NON-TECHNICAL CORE COMPETENCIES

As aviators we are extremely familiar with standards, SOPs, operations manuals and training manuals. These worthy documents tell us what is expected of us and how we should go about achieving it. They give us chapter and verse, often in great detail, on how to carry out a range of activities from the normal to the abnormal, and are updated and amended on a regular basis.

Should you feel like ditching one day, then some document will tell you how to do it in black and white, complete with the odd picture.

What is often missing is the equivalent for non-technical standards and I will now try and remedy this omission. It is also further explanation as to why this section of the book goes into more detail than the technical and operational. I offer you a set of standards, which have now been translated into core competencies and performance indicators (to fit in with current terminology), which have been accepted by many pilots and trainers, plus some ideas as to how you might achieve these. They were adopted as the basis for the remaining 5 ICAO Core Competencies, but I will use the ones that LMQ and many operators are currently using.

The core competencies and their performance indicators are designed to achieve the following:

- To give crews something tangible to work toward.
- To break down the subject into clear and understandable actions.
- To be comprehensive so that no action that affects performance is missing.
- To reflect best practice amongst current professionals.
- To be simple and easy to observe.
- To enable an assessment to be as objective as possible.

How the Non-Technical Competencies were developed

The following competencies were developed by asking over a thousand experienced professionals what they think safe, effective and efficient people do. The actions listed below were those that were consistently mentioned. To refine some of these actions, we then observed good operators at work. Not only in their professional role but also when undertaking training exercises, which is when there is an opportunity to put them through their paces. We tried to identify what they did that made them so effective, and although the list may not have covered everything, it is good enough for most people to use as a reference. We also made the competencies as comprehensive as possible so that no key part was missed out, and then we left it to individuals to use them as they wished.

Furthermore, to confirm whether these competencies were valid, particularly as a basis for improving flight safety, we then looked at some of the key accidents to discover if any of the performance indicators were missing and if their omission may have been a contributory cause. What we found was that in every case, most of the performance indicators had not been followed, and in the following chapters some examples are interspersed with more detail explanation of each of the competencies. The reverse was also found to be true with the successful exemplary incidents such as Qantas QF32.

The Non-Technical Core Competencies

There are 5 non-technical core competencies: communications, leadership and teamworking, workload management, situation awareness, and problem solving and decision-making.

A word of caution may be necessary here. Although I recommend that we strive to continually improve what we do, if every time you went flying you tried religiously to follow these, then a couple of chaps in white coats will come and take you away! Nevertheless, I think if you gradually work on improving them and notice the problems that occur when you fail to meet them, then over time they will become second nature.

Non-Technical Competencies

Observable Performance Indicators

Communications – Crew members:

- Know what, where, how much, how and to whom they need to communicate.
- Ensure the receiver is ready and able to receive the information.
- Pass messages and information clearly, accurately, timely and adequately.
- Check the other person has the correct understanding when passing important information.
- Listen actively, patiently and demonstrate understanding when receiving information.

- Ask relevant and effective questions, and offer suggestions.
- Use appropriate body language, eye contact and tone, and read other people's accurately.
- Are receptive to other people's views and willing to compromise.

Leadership and Teamworking – Crew members:

- Agree and are clear on the team's objectives and members' roles.
- Are friendly, enthusiastic, motivating and considerate of others.
- Use initiative, give direction and take responsibility when required.
- Anticipate other crew members' needs and carry out instructions as directed.
- Are open and honest about thoughts, concerns and intentions.
- Give and receive criticism and praise well, and admit mistakes.
- Confidently do and say what is important to them.
- Demonstrate respect, empathy and tolerance for other people.
- Involve others in planning and share activities fairly, appropriate to abilities.

Workload management – Crew members:

- Are calm, relaxed, careful, not impulsive and consider implications of their actions.
- Prepare, prioritise and schedule tasks effectively.
- Manage time available efficiently to complete tasks.
- Offer and accept assistance, delegate if necessary and call for help early.
- Monitor, cross-check and review actions conscientiously.
- Concentrate on one thing at a time and ensure tasks are completed.
- Manage interruptions, distractions, variations and failures effectively.
- Follow procedures appropriately and consistently.

Situation awareness – Crew members:

- Are aware of what the aircraft and its systems are doing.
- Are aware of where the aircraft is and its environment.
- Are aware of the condition of the people involved in the operation, including passengers.
- Keep track of time and fuel.
- Recognise what is likely to happen, plan, make pre-decisions and stay ahead of the situation.
- Identify threats to the safety of the aircraft and people, and take appropriate action.

Problem solving and Decision making – Crew members

- Identify and verify why things have gone wrong and do not jump to conclusions or make uninformed assumptions.
- Seek accurate and adequate information from appropriate resources.
- Persevere working through a problem.
- Use and agree an appropriate and timely decision making process.
- Agree essential and desirable criteria and prioritise.
- Consider as many options as practicable.
- Make decisions when they need to, review and change if required.
- Consider risks but do not take unnecessary risks.

Accident and incident analysis

The following table includes part of the original analysis undertaken to validate the competencies and includes several of the accidents described in this book, indicating where there may have been gaps in the non-technical competencies by one or more members of the crew, based on the accident reports and cockpit voice recordings. The analysis is not intended to indicate probable cause, or purport to explain the accident, but just to endorse the relevance of the competencies in improving flight safety.

Accident/Incident	AIR BLUE	TENERIFE	MT EREBUS	PORTLAND	SIOUX CITY	JAVA	QANTAS	AF 447	KEGWORTH	HELIOS
Communications										
Know what, where, how much, how and to whom they need to communicate	X	X	X	X	✓	✓	✓	X	X	X
Ensure the recipient is ready and able to receive the information	X	X	X	X	✓	✓	✓	X	X	–
Pass messages and information clearly, accurately, timely and adequately	X	X	X	X	✓	✓	✓	X	X	–
Check the other person has the correct understanding when passing important information	X	X	X	–	✓	✓	✓	X	X	X
Listen actively, patiently and demonstrate understanding when receiving information	X	X	X	X	✓	✓	✓	X	X	X
Ask relevant and effective questions and offer suggestions	–	X	X	X	✓	✓	✓	X	X	X
Use appropriate body language, eye contact and tone and read other people's accurately	X	X	–	–	✓	✓	✓	–	–	–
Are receptive to other people's views and willing to compromise	X	X	X	X	✓	✓	✓	–	–	–
Leadership & Teamworking										
Agree and are clear on the team's objectives and members' roles	X	X	X	–	✓	✓	✓	X	–	–
Are friendly, enthusiastic, motivating and considerate of others	X	–	–	–	✓	✓	✓	-	–	–
Use initiative, give direction and take responsibility when required	X	X	X	X	✓	✓	✓	X	–	X
Anticipate other crew members' needs and carry out instructions as directed	–	–	–	X	✓	✓	✓	X	–	–
Are open and honest about thoughts, feelings and intentions	–	X	X	X	✓	✓	✓	X	–	–

	AIR BLUE	TENERIFE	MT EREBUS	PORTLAND	SIOUX CITY	JAVA	QANTAS	AF 447	KEGWORTH	HELIOS
Give and receive criticism and praise well, and admit mistakes	X	X	X	X	✓	✓	✓	–	–	–
Confidently do and say what is important to them	X	X	X	X	✓	✓	✓	X	X	X
Demonstrate respect, empathy and tolerance for other people	X	–	–	–	✓	✓	✓	–	–	–
Involve others in planning and share activities fairly, appropriate to abilities	X	X	X	X	✓	✓	✓	–	X	–
Workload Management										
Are calm, relaxed, careful and not impulsive	X	X	–	–	✓	✓	✓	X	X	–
Prepare, prioritise and schedule tasks effectively	X	X	X	X	✓	✓	✓	–	–	–
Manage time efficiently to complete tasks	X	X	–	X	✓	✓	✓	–	X	–
Offer and accept assistance, delegate if necessary and call for help early	X	X	–	–	✓	✓	✓	X	–	–
Cross-check, monitor and review actions conscientiously	X	X	X	X	✓	✓	✓	X	X	X
Follow procedures appropriately and consistently	X	X	X	–	✓	✓	✓	X	X	X
Concentrate on one thing at a time and ensure tasks are completed	X	X	–	–	✓	✓	✓	X	–	–
Manage interruptions, distractions, variations and failures effectively	X	–	–	–	✓	✓	✓	X	–	–
Situation Awareness										
Are aware of what the aircraft and its systems are doing	X	–	–	X	✓	✓	✓	X	X	X
Are aware of where the aircraft is and its environment	X	X	X	X	✓	✓	✓	X	–	X

	AIR BLUE	TENERIFE	MT EREBUS	PORTLAND	SIOUX CITY	JAVA	QANTAS	AF 447	KEGWORTH	HELIOS
Are aware of the condition of the people involved in the operation including passengers	X	X	–	–	✓	✓	✓	–	–	–
Recognise what is likely to happen, plan, make pre-decisions and stay ahead of the situation	X	X	X	X	✓	✓	✓	X	–	–
Keep track of time and fuel	–	–	–	X	✓	✓	✓	–	–	–
Identify threats to the safety of the aircraft and people, and take appropriate action	X	X	X	X	✓	✓	✓	X	–	–
Problem solving & Decision making										
Identify and verify why things have gone wrong and do not jump to conclusions or make uninformed assumptions	–	–	–	–	✓	✓	✓	X	X	X
Seek accurate and adequate information from appropriate resources	X	–	–	–	✓	✓	✓	X	X	X
Persevere working through a problem	–	–	–	–	✓	✓	✓	X	X	X
Use and agree an appropriate and timely decision making process	–	–	X	X	✓	✓	✓	–	–	–
Agree essential and desirable criteria and prioritise	X	–	X	X	✓	✓	–	–	–	–
Consider as many options as practicable	–	–	–	–	✓	✓	✓	–	–	X
Make decisions when they need to, review and change if required	X	X	–	X	✓	✓	✓	–	–	–
Consider risks but do not take unnecessary risks	X	X	X	–	✓	✓	✓	–	–	–

Some of the accidents and incidents listed in the table are described below, plus a few others that have been similarly analysed. The Sioux City, Qantas A380, and Java incidents that have been described earlier are also included to illustrate how the presence of all the competencies results in a positive outcome.

CASE STUDY

Air Blue

On the 28th July 2010, Air Blue Flight 202 departed Karachi for Islamabad. During the flight the report suggested that the relationship between the two pilots had deteriorated. On the approach to Islamabad the aircraft flew an ILS approach to RW30 followed by a visual circling approach to RW12. The captain instructed the co-pilot to insert unauthorized way-points in the FMS and descended below the MDA. The captain also did not respond to calls from the tower inquiring as to whether he was visual and failed to activate the heading mode on the autopilot when wanting to turn. Even though the crew had 21 GPWS warnings, the captain ignored repeated calls from the co-pilot to pull up or turn, and the aircraft flew into hills 9 miles northeast of the airfield with the loss of 152 lives.

Air Blue A321 AP-BJB prior to the accident (Konstantin von Wedelstaedt)

Air New Zealand DC-10 Mount Erebus

On the 28th November 1979 an Air New Zealand DC-10 took off from Auckland for a sightseeing trip to the Antarctic. Included in the crew was a guide, whose role was to provide commentary for the passengers and who was not involved in the navigation of the aircraft. They flew over the Ross Sea at 18,000ft intending to overfly the USAF base at McMurdo, but due to a navigation error in the INS were actually 25 miles east of their planned track. They tried to establish their exact position but were unsuccessful, as can be discerned from the CVR below. Even though they had a DME ground station and radar coverage from McMurdo, they descended down to 1,500ft in marginal VMC conditions and flew into the side of Mount Erebus while initiating a climb. A USAF Starlifter following behind maintained altitude until its crew had confirmed their position with the ground station and had been identified by radar control, and landed without a problem. The probable cause of the accident in the official report was:

The decision of the captain to continue the flight at low level toward an area of poor surface and horizon definition when the crew was not certain of their position and the subsequent inability to detect the rising terrain which intercepted the aircraft's flight path.

The following is the final part of the CVR transcript:

FE	Where's Erebus in relation to us at the moment?
Guide	Left, about 20 or 25 miles.
FO	Yep.
FE	I'm just thinking of any high ground in the area, that's all.
Guide	I think it'll be left.
FE	Yes, I reckon about here.
Guide	Yes ... no, no, I don't really know.
Guide	That's the edge.
CA	Yes, OK. Probably is further anyway.
FO	It's not too bad.
Guide	I reckon Bird's through here and Ross Island there. Erebus should be there.

CA	Actually, these conditions don't look very good at all, do they?
Guide	No they don't.
Guide	That looks like the edge of Ross Island there.
FE	I don't like this.
CA	Have you got anything from him?
FO	No
CA	We're 26 miles north. We'll have to climb out of this.
Guide	You can see Ross Island? Fine.
FO	You're clear to turn right. There's no high ground if you do a one eighty.
CA	No ... negative.
GPWS	Whoop, whoop. Pull up. Whoop whoop.
FE	Five hundred feet.
GPWS	Pull up.
FE	Four hundred feet.
GPWS	Whoop, whoop. Pull up. Whoop whoop. Pull up.
CA	Go-around power please.

Sound of impact.

The wreckage of the DC10 on the slopes of Mt. Erebus

Portland

On the 28th December 1978 a United Airways DC-8 was making its final approach to Portland, Oregon, when it had a malfunction with the under-carriage. The crew could not determine if it was fully down and locked, so the captain ordered the cabin crew to prepare for an emergency landing. In the meantime the DC-8 orbited to the south of the airfield while the crew tried to see if there was anything else they could do. The captain was keen to ensure that the cabin was ready for the landing and delayed the final approach until the cabin was secure. However, the aircraft's engines flamed out due to fuel starvation and it crashed 6nm short of the runway threshold. The fuel usage rate while circling at low altitude was higher

The United DC-8 after landing in trees short of the runway at Portland

than they expected and they ran out of fuel on final approach. The first officer and flight engineer had made comments about the fuel state, but it would appear that the captain had not registered the severity of the problem. The probable cause, according to the report was:

The failure of the captain to monitor properly the aircraft's fuel state and to properly respond to the low fuel state and the crewmember's advisories regarding fuel state. This resulted in fuel exhaustion to all engines. His inattention resulted from preoccupation with a landing gear malfunction and preparations for a possible landing emergency. Contributing to the accident was the failure of the other two flight crew members either to fully comprehend the criticality of the fuel state or to successfully communicate their concern to the captain.

Kegworth

On the 8th January 1989 a British Midland Boeing 737 en route from Heathrow to Belfast suffered an engine failure climbing through FL280. The symptoms they experienced were severe vibration and a smell of smoke in the cockpit. Conclusions from the accident report were as follows:

The crew shut down the No.2 engine after a fan blade had fractured in the No.1 engine. This engine subsequently suffered a major thrust loss due to secondary fan damage after power had been increased during the final approach to land. The following factors contributed to the incorrect response of the flight crew:

The combination of heavy engine vibration, noise, shuddering and an associated smell of fire were outside their training and experience.

- They reacted to the initial engine problem prematurely and in a way that was contrary to their training.
- They did not assimilate the indications on the engine instrument display before they throttled back the No.2 engine.
- As the No.2 engine was throttled back, the noise and shuddering associated with the surging of the No.1 engine ceased, persuading them that they had correctly identified the defective engine.

- They were not informed of the flames which had emanated from the No.1 engine and which had been observed by many on board, including three cabin attendants in the aft cabin.

In some respects this supports the argument for having too much knowledge, as the crew made some assumptions rather than reading what was in front of them.

The British Midland B737 just short of the runway near Kegworth

Tenerife

On the 27th March 1977 a KLM Boeing 747 and a Pan Am Boeing 747 had been diverted, along with many other aircraft, to Tenerife in the Canary Islands. After waiting for most of the afternoon for weather at their original destinations to clear, the various aircraft began to takeoff from Tenerife. However, because of a late decision by the KLM captain to refuel, the two 747s were delayed by another 45 minutes.

Finally, the two aircraft were told to back track down the runway and take-off in turn. The KLM led the way, followed by the Pan Am, and when it reached the end of the runway executed a 180° turn and prepared for take-off. However, the Pan Am was still taxiing slowly down the runway and was unseen by either the tower or the KLM crew, as hill fog had begun to cover the airport; the fog had been steadily reducing the RVR to the minimum allowed for take-off at Tenerife. Keen to ensure they kept within crew duty time and were not caught out by the fog, Captain van Zanten began his take-off roll without take-off clearance.

The following extract from the CVR in the KLM cockpit shows what happened just before the two aircraft collided.

Picture taken of both B747s waiting at Tenerife before the accident

FO	KLM 4805 is now ready for take-off and we're waiting for our ATC clearance.
TWR	KLM 8705 you are cleared to the Papa Beacon climb to ...
FO	Ah roger, sir, we're cleared to the Papa ... and we're now (at take-off).
CA	We gaan. (We're going.)
TWR	Stand by for take-off, I will call you.
PA	And we're still taxiing down the runway, the Clipper. 1736. (The above Pan Am and TWR transmissions caused a shrill noise in KLM cockpit.)
TWR	Roger alpha 1736, report when runway clear.
PA	OK, we'll report when we're clear.
FE	Is hij er niet af dan? (Is he not clear then?)
CA	Wat zeg je? (What do you say?)
FE	Is hij er niet af, die Pan American?
CA	Jawel. (Yes.)
Collision	

CASE STUDY

Dryden

On the 10th March 1989 an Air Ontario Fokker F-28 departed Thunder Bay about one hour behind schedule. The aircraft landed at Dryden and was refuelled with one engine running because of an unserviceable APU. There were further delays as a light aircraft made an emergency landing, and during this period a snow shower passed over the airfield. Although a layer of snow had accumulated on the wings, no de-icing was done because de-icing with either engine running was prohibited by both Fokker and Air Ontario. Since no external power unit was available at Dryden, the engines couldn't be restarted in case of engine shutdown on the ground. The crew had had a long day and were under pressure to complete the flight as soon as possible. Passengers in the cabin had expressed concern to the cabin crew about the accumulation of snow on the wings, but the message never reached the pilots. The aircraft started its take-off roll using the slush-covered runway but settled back after the first rotation and lifted off for the second time at the 5,700ft point of the 6,000ft runway. No altitude was gained and the aircraft settled into a nose-high attitude, striking trees. The aircraft crashed and came to rest in a wooded area past the runway end, and caught fire. The investigation concluded that:

The pilot in command must bear responsibility for the decision to take-off at Dryden on the day in question. However, it is equally clear that the air transportation system failed him by allowing him to be placed in a situation where he did not have all the necessary tools that should have supported him in making the proper decision.

The F28 after failing to get airborne at Dryden

COMMUNICATIONS

The following sections explain each competency performance indicator in more detail. In some cases a particular accident has been highlighted to give an example of the omission of the indicator, although I am not suggesting it is the main omission, or indeed the only one.

Failures of communication are present in most incidents, accidents and wastage of resources, and they probably also contribute to most of the stress and pressure that we live under. We have almost become resigned to the fact that 'communications failures' will occur and there is not much we can do about it, particularly as it is always someone else's fault, of course.

Communication is the principal activity for making sure that information is passed from one human being to another. Living an isolated existence, a person probably has little need for communication, but the dynamic, inter-connected world most of us live in demands that good communications are critical to our existence.

However, communications is another area where definition is required. For a skill that causes or contributes to causing most accidents, it is rarely clearly set out what pilots are required to do and how they should do it. Statements such as 'Your communication skills were poor' or 'You can't communicate' do not really help someone to improve. But they could learn to demonstrate good communication skills if they understood and achieved agreed, clear and observable performance indicators such as the following.

The communications performance indicators

Crew members know what, where, how much, how and to whom they need to communicate. This means giving people the right amount of information, enough but not too much, and ensuring it is relevant to the situation, otherwise they will be confused. As we can normally keep only about seven different pieces of information in our short-term memory, it is pointless to give someone more than this, as they will replace the earlier data or probably end up not registering any of it. We must also ensure that we give information to the people who need to know. We often say, 'I didn't think you needed to know.' Getting into the habit of thinking about 'who needs to know' the information that you have, is something most of us need to work on. Conversely, if others don't need to know something, then they don't need to know, and shouldn't be burdened with unnecessary information. Thinking about how you will communicate and what is the most appropriate medium is also important in ensuring an accurate message is transferred, and finally, the above applies of course to written communication as well.

Guam

On the 6th August 6 1997, Korean Air Flight 801 was conducting a night time approach to Guam runway 06L. Even though the glide slope was unavailable an ILS with VOR approach was flown. The aeroplane had been cleared to land on runway 6L at Guam International Airport but had descended 800ft below the prescribed altitude and struck the 70ft Nimitz Hill at a height of 650ft. It crashed in a jungle valley about 3 miles south west of the airport, breaking up and bursting into flames. The National Transportation Safety Board determined that the probable cause of the accident was the captain's failure to adequately brief and execute the non-precision approach, and the first officer's and flight engineer's failure to effectively monitor and cross check the captain's execution of the approach.

The Korean Air Boeing 747 on Nimitz Hill in Guam

CASE STUDY

They ensure the receiver is ready and able to receive the information. A person who is not in a position to receive information, because they are busy, distracted, upset or unwilling, may not get any information at all, or will most likely get the wrong message. So it is pointless trying to communicate with someone when they are not ready to receive, such as if they are on the radio or studying a chart. This is most commonly found when people are having arguments, and everyone is talking at once. Even though a person is looking at you, they still may not be ready to receive any information if their mind is elsewhere.

They pass messages and information clearly, accurately, timely and adequately. It is important to be as clear and unambiguous as possible, to be accurate, and to tell people at the right time. There is no point saying, 'I forgot to tell you', or 'I meant to tell you earlier', or giving them information too far in advance. How often do we say to ourselves 'I must tell so and so later', and then forget? Also make sure you give them all the information, not half the story, and avoid missing out things that may not seem significant to you, but could be to them. The game of 'Chinese whispers' only works because people just add or take away words without consideration.

They check the other person has the correct understanding when passing important information. Try this at home. Give someone some relatively detailed information and then ask them to back what you have said. You will be surprised how often they get some detail wrong. I think this happens because people are either not fully concentrating or they are making assumptions about what you are saying. We are reluctant to check understanding because the person might not have been listening, and then it all gets far too embarrassing.

They listen actively and patiently, and demonstrate understanding when receiving information. Concentrate when you are listening, allow the other person time to fully communicate their message, and then give them confidence that you have got it by demonstrating what you have understood. Again, mainly because people do not always say what they mean, you will be surprised how often you are corrected. This is a habit we do naturally with ATC instructions, so there is no reason why we can't extend it to other communications.

They ask relevant and effective questions, and offer suggestions. Communications often break down or cease because not enough questions are asked, or the questions are not effective enough. It is important to ask questions to be clear both for yourself and for the other person about what is happening. Along with this, it is important to offer suggestions rather than keep them to yourself and then say afterwards, 'Actually it did occur to me beforehand that we should have...'

They use appropriate body language, eye contact and tone and read other people's accurately. As described later in the book, body language, eye contact and tone are fundamental to good communications and often the cause of communications failures. It is not just what you say or do – but the way that you say or do it. This performance indicator also includes the ability to read other's body language, so you can react if they are tired, confused, concerned or stressed.

They are receptive to other people's views and willing to compromise. If you only rely on the information you have in your head, then you will have a limited knowledge base. Using just one other person's experience could double what you have, but it is of no use unless you are open and receptive to what they are suggesting. Furthermore, if they feel you are receptive to their viewpoint it is more likely they will agree with what you are saying as well. Otherwise, while you are talking they won't be listening, because they will be trying to work out why you don't understand, and developing a different way to tell you. Although you do not always need to compromise it is important that you are willing to do so.

This picture was taken shortly after the collision at Tenerife; this tragedy and the loss of almost 600 lives could have been avoided by the crew using all of the above communication standards

Why we don't communicate well

To improve our ability to communicate, we need first to identify why we don't do it well, and then to learn some ways to overcome those hurdles. Therefore, let's begin with some reasons why we communicate poorly.

Behavioural:

We can't be bothered.
We don't like the person.
We don't respect the person.
We don't have time.
We don't trust the person.
We want to hold the information to ourselves.
We are fearful of saying anything.
We don't want to look stupid.
We are shy or under-confident.

Technical or skill-based:

We don't understand the information ourselves.
We assume we don't need to as the other person already knows.
We don't realise we have to.
We forget.
We don't listen well.
We lack the skill to be clear.
We don't believe it is important.
We think the information is irrelevant.
We miss non-verbal clues.
Our own non-verbal messages confuse the other person.

With so many reasons, it is not surprising that the world is full of communication failures. The trick therefore is to identify what causes these and to put in place solutions to prevent or at least minimise their occurrence. I have found by dividing the list into reasons that might be considered 'behavioural' and into reasons that might be considered 'technical or skill-based', it becomes a lot easier to manage the problem. I believe the behavioural reasons can be overcome by people having the right attitude and behaving appropriately, with self-respect and respect for others; and I think the technical reasons can be overcome if people use the following communications toolkit.

Communications toolkit

Here is a communications toolkit that some organisations have introduced and used effectively. The first step is to identify the triggers for you to communicate, and there are three events:

If a problem has arisen or things are not going to plan.
If a decision has been made, either yours or someone else's.
If you have received information either orally or in documentation.

The memory response to these triggers are the following vital actions:

Ask yourself: 'Who needs to know?' Then take full responsibility for transferring the message completely, accurately, clearly and timely to the people who need to know. Use the following process to communicate.

Transmitting

It is your responsibility they get the right message.

Tune in
Get their attention.
Check the other person's position (ask if they are ready to receive and a brief idea of what you are going to tell them).

Deliver
Tell them what you need to tell them. Be clear and specific.
Use appropriate body language and tone.

Check understanding
Ask open questions, unless you are confident they have demonstrated understanding. Note their body language.
Reach agreement or confirm.

Receiving

It is your responsibility you receive the right message.

Tune in
Look interested.
Tell them your position. Do you have time to listen properly?

Receive
LISTEN
Demonstrate understanding
Tell them what you understand. Show agreement.

Key communications skills

To understand and be understood, there are four key skills that people need. They are: Being clear and specific. Listening skills. Questioning skills. Non-verbal skills.

Being clear and specific

The ability to be clear and specific is lost on most of us who prefer a different approach – I think we call it waffling – but even though brevity is desirable it should not be at the expense of being clear and accurate. However, it is a skill than can be learned and just requires practice. Here are three steps that might help:

First: Ask yourself exactly what the message is that you want them to receive. Include everything that is relevant in this, such as perhaps your feelings and your understanding of their feelings.

Second: Construct your sentence.

Third: Take out unnecessary words and amend if at all confusing.

As a simple example, let's say you would like someone to check your fuel calculation. You could say 'Can you check the fuel?' This is short but possibly unclear – the bluntness may send the wrong message. Does it mean they have to monitor the refuelling, or calculate the fuel figures from scratch, or test the quality? It is confusing as they have just noticed you doing the figures, so why are you asking them? Or are you testing whether they can do it correctly? Finally, it gives them an opportunity to be really naughty and reply, 'Yes, I can.' – ('But I won't'). So, check – what is the message you want them to receive? Well, you want them to review the figures in case you have made a mistake, but you also want them to know that you realise they are busy.

So you might say, 'Simon, old bean, far from it for me to interrupt your extremely hectic workload, but would you be so awfully kind as to cast your beady eye over these scribbles here and see what you make of them as I really have a tendency to lose the plot, because the last thing we want is to run out of fuel, which nearly happened to me in 1994 when ...'

Finally, let's do some editing and say, 'Simon, when you have time, will you check my fuel calculations in case I have made a mistake?'

Listening skills

There is a saying that hearing is done with your ears and listening with your mind, and I think what it means is that although you may have heard something, you may not have registered the information.

Often called active listening, it is a vitally important skill and one whose omission often plays a part in incidents and accidents. I know that a failure to listen was at the heart of most of the thousands of errors I have made. It is something that requires concentration, and I am convinced that we can only concentrate on one thing at a time. We may be able to do several things at once but we can only concentrate on one.

Try listening to something interesting on the radio or TV and reading the paper at the same time. Can't be done. You lose the thread and end up painfully flicking backwards and forwards until you either put the paper down or turn off the radio.

Another example of this is when someone is talking directly to you but your mind has begun to wander. You start thinking of what you are going to do later, or what the weather might be like at the weekend, and then you suddenly remember something you have forgotten to do. You are responding in the appropriate manner, a nod here, an 'Aha' there, good eye contact and the customary tilt of the head, but after a while you have absolutely no idea what they are talking about – not a clue.

And when asked the inevitable, 'What do you think?' you desperately begin to scrabble at sounds that are slowly fading into the ether for some inkling of the subject that you have appeared to be listening so well to. The clever response of course is, 'I couldn't agree more', with a hearty slap on the arm and a big smile. The look of dismay on your fellow conversationalist is followed by your discovery that their last sentence was in fact, 'Everyone thinks I am useless, what do you think?'!

Here is an easy to use acronym – **LISTEN** – that may help as a memory jogger.

Look interested

Have good eye contact, and that means look them in the eye. Not around the face, over their shoulder, or focused halfway between you and them, but squarely in the eye, just like your grandmother used to tell you. Nod, and develop facial expressions that are consistent with what they are saying.

However, don't overdo it, although you will find that if you are genuinely listening this comes naturally. Don't fidget, look at your watch, out of the window or generally become distracted. Above all, avoid falling asleep.

Interact with questions

Ask the odd question that demonstrates you are listening and helps them to clarify what they are saying, or possibly expand on the subject. Making a comment that you can understand what they are saying or feeling is also helpful.

Stay tuned

Don't allow the talker to drift off the subject and digress, but bring them back to where they were. Certainly don't take over the conversation or develop your own agenda.

Test understanding

Check that you have understood what they are saying. This can be done in two ways. You can paraphrase what they have said using your own words and thoughts, which lets them know the message you have received. Or you can use their exact words back to them. Either way they will correct you if it is not quite what they said or meant.

Evaluate the message

Read between the lines and try to decipher exactly what the message is that they are conveying to you. See whether the words match the tune as displayed by their tone and body language. Also think about the words they have chosen and when they have said them. There are thousands of words in the dictionary, yet people pluck out words which on closer examination are out of context or strange; or they wait for a particular moment to say something and therein lies the message.

Neutralise your thoughts and feelings

Put your assumptions, preconceptions and prejudices to one side. Yes, yes, of course we know what they are going to say – but on this occasion it might be a different message. Don't allow these thoughts to block your listening. Furthermore, if you are angry, nervous or frustrated, don't allow these or other feelings to distract you from listening fully to what is being said. As an indicator, if ever in a conversation the other person says, 'Don't worry, I will tell you later', then you have just been caught not listening.

Questioning skills

Questioning is another fundamental skill at which few people excel. Although effective questioning may seem to be just the domain of lawyers, policeman, journalists and mothers, actually the ability to ask simple, non-threatening and unambiguous questions is at the heart of good communications. A lot of young children are extraordinary good at it. I am sure we all have amusing stories of the questions our children have asked, and one I remember was during a car journey. The toddler asked if he could have a drink, but we had run out of rations and were in motorway traffic.

'Can I have something to drink?'
'Sorry, we haven't anything left.'
'But I am thirsty, why can't you get some more?'
'Because we can't stop now, so you will just have to suffer.'
Long pause ...
'How do I suffer?'

I don't know when it was that we stopped asking good questions. Probably at school after being told not to for the hundredth time, or possibly because we learned how to talk a lot rather than listen. Questioning just gives the other person the opportunity to talk, which is the last thing we want when we are on a roll. I constantly struggle to find the right question, and this is because I am either afraid to upset the other person or that I am only trying to get the answer that I want. The principles of being clear and specific apply here also. Check with yourself:

What exactly is it that you want an answer to?
How can you ensure they answer only that question?

Adopt the 'comedian sketch' test. Is your question likely to develop into this:

'Why did you do that?'
– 'Do what?'
'What you did.'
– 'What did I do?'
'You know.'
– 'No I don't'.
'Why are you being difficult?'
– 'Why are you?'
'Because you did what you did.'

There are many accidents where either a confusing question or a statement that should have been a question were significant contributory causes. Moreover a good question could have actually prevented the crew having the accident at all.

In the Tenerife accident the flight engineer asked the captain twice, 'Is hij er niet af dan?' which, roughly translated, means, 'Is he not off then?' I can only assume that the captain and first officer did not understand the question as intended, because it is unlikely they really wanted to collide with another 747. So possibly what might have helped would have been to ask 'Is that Pan American 747 still on the runway?'

Similarly, in the Erebus accident, if any member of the crew had asked, 'Does anyone know exactly where we are?' and if the answer was 'Yes', followed by, 'Where?' and then 'How do you know?', then this might have prompted a discussion and they might not have descended when they did.

Types of questions

There are several types of questions that we can use (the type is defined by the response, as some are similar):

Open questions

These questions begin with the words What, Why and How. The response to these questions can be anything, and they are used to start a discussion, or to get a fuller response. Open questions are often far more effective at ensuring you get accurate information, but also for ensuring nothing is missed. An example would be, 'What do you think we should do?'

Direct questions

These questions begin with What, When, Where, and Who. The response is some specific bit of information that you are seeking. An example would be, 'What time is it?'

Closed questions

These questions can result in just a 'Yes', 'No' or 'Don't know.' answer. They are used to clarify or to add structure to a conversation, as a long list of open questions might feel a bit interrogative. An example would be, 'Have you done the walk round?'

Probing questions

These questions are used to elicit more detailed information or to get a better understanding of someone's thoughts. The ultimate probing question is of course, 'Why?' Another example would be, 'What do you mean by that?'

Summarising questions

These questions are used to bring a conversation to a close, to check understanding or to confirm an agreement. An example would be, 'What have we agreed?'

You should try to avoid:

Leading questions: 'You did do that didn't you? Wouldn't you agree that ...?'. Although they can be used as a gentler way to give an instruction, or checking understanding.

Multiple questions: Several at once.

Ambiguous questions: Those that are confusing and unclear.

Non-verbal communications skills

Popularly known as body language, this is an absolutely vital subject and is at the root of many a misunderstanding. Some research has demonstrated that a message is divided into words, tone and body language, and their relative importance to the understanding of the message are 7, 37 and 60 per cent, respectively. I am not sure I agree with the figures, but if it shows that non-verbal communications are important, then that will do for me. I think there are two parts of the subject and they are of equal significance. The first part is managing your own body language, and the second part is reading other people's.

Managing your body language

Many people are perplexed as to why they are misunderstood. They often say things like, 'All I said was ...'. But it is not what you say, it is the way that you say it. We are very lazy at managing our body language, tone and facial expressions, particularly in Northern Europe and North America. People from Latin countries and from those further East and South tend to use more expressions and gesticulate more. In Britain we actually get formal training in this, and are regularly told from an early age to maintain a stiff upper lip, whatever this means you are supposed to do.

But I will repeat, it is very, very important not only to say what you think, but think about how you are saying it. This does not mean putting on an act, but rather trying to match your tone, expression and body language to the true message you are trying to convey. If you don't believe me, just think about all the influential people you have known in your life; those people who we are happy to do favours for, who get listened to and who are generally respected and popular. Think about how they communicate with others and I am pretty sure you will not remember someone with a straight face, stiff body and monotone voice.

Reading other people's body language

This is an area fraught with danger. There are multiple books illustrating all sorts of weird and wonderful things – when a person does this it means that, and when a person does that it means this. Take these with a large pinch of salt or else you will find yourself at worst in a heap of trouble, and at best miscommunicating with a lot of people.

Unlike animals, who have very consistent body language, human beings vary enormously. This is because of many things. We feel differently about things because of our completely different past experiences; the strength of our feelings varies, and our bodies will react in accordance with those feelings. We are all different shapes; we have had different illnesses and injuries; and we enjoy different levels of fitness. Therefore our muscles and joints will adopt differing positions depending on what is comfortable.

Our conditioning and learned behaviour is a function of the other people we have been exposed to and this is different for each person; our cultures are different and so is the amount of exposure we have had to other cultures. And finally we get into habits – when I touch my nose it does not mean I am lying, it just means I want to pick my nose! Nevertheless, I cannot stress enough the importance of reading other people's body language. It is a vital part of the message they are communicating, and because most people are very good at trying to hide their thoughts and feelings it is very difficult to be able to do accurately. So how do we learn to do it? Try the following steps:

Observe carefully – This is where I believe men differ from women. Men tend not to observe others too closely when they are communicating with them and thus have far less experience of the art, whereas women tend to study the other person very carefully. You will notice that women are more likely to communicate facing each other, whereas men will be more to the side. This is not because men want to avoid conflict or some other theory – women just want front row seats. Now, their skill in reading body language may be because of the anthropology associated with nests, nurturing infants and maintaining harmony, but let's not get over-analytical about it – they just do it. It is sometimes referred to as women's intuition, but actually it is just that they have many more thousands of hours of practice in reading body language compared with men.

Don't assume – What you see may not necessarily mean what it looks like. For me the best example is when people are smiling and looking happy – they may not be. In fact they are often nervous, uncomfortable or embarrassed. Just look at a queue for the white-knuckle ride at the theme park and you will see lots of apparently happy people! Also, someone who has their arms folded and legs crossed is not being defensive or disagreeing with what you are saying: it is just a typical comfortable position.

Check it out – If they are talking, ask questions to confirm if what you see is consistent with what they are saying. And if you are talking and notice a change in body language, just re-run what you have said in your mind, and you will often find that you have used a contentious word or phrase. Ask them what their thoughts are which gives them an opportunity of telling you verbally what they may be telling you non-verbally.

Look for changes – Although we can't identify what one particular gesture or position means, we can however notice changes, and these can be quite telling or at least give us an alert that the other person's thought process may have changed. Again, the golden rule is: check it out.

LEADERSHIP AND TEAMWORKING

The leadership and teamworking performance indicators

Crew members agree and are clear on the team's objectives and members' roles

A team can only function well if everyone is clear on what the team is trying to achieve, how it is going to achieve it and who is doing what. When members of a team have different opinions about the team's objectives and do not agree on how the team will go about the task, then it will operate ineffectively and inefficiently. Also, when team members have this clarity, they are able to think for themselves independently and are committed to the direction the team is going. Team members must be clear on what their role is and what they are responsible for. Good leadership is about trusting people to take responsibility for their role and allowing them to get on and do it.

They are friendly, enthusiastic, motivating and considerate of others
I am often asked if this is relevant to professional work, especially being a pilot, and my response is quite clear. Given the option I think everyone would prefer to work with colleagues who are friendly and enthusiastic. I think we also prefer to work with people who are interested in our work, encourage us, and are considerate of our needs and the problems that we may have. I think people who are stern, only focused on the task, inconsiderate in their actions, and expect everyone to be totally committed to the job, are unprofessional and a safety risk, because they put pressure on others, as well as being distracting.

They use initiative, give direction and take responsibility when required
There are times when if we can see what needs to be done, we need to do it. If others are not yet clear and time is short, then we need to give direction and take responsibility for managing the task. This does not mean we shout and scream orders. Giving direction cannot be done in isolation and must be balanced with other performance indicators as described above and below. An example of this would be if the captain is fixated on one aspect of an approach, does not notice that the speed is high or acknowledge warnings, and the co-pilot realises a go-around is inevitable. He or she just needs to clearly and firmly call 'Go-around', and be prepared to take control if the captain fails to respond.

CASE STUDY

Toronto
On the 2nd August 2005, an Air France Airbus A340 departed Paris for a scheduled flight to Toronto. Weather conditions were poor with heavy thunderstorms and rain as the aircraft approached Toronto under control of the co-pilot who was the handling pilot. The crew were cleared to descend to 5,000ft and to reduce their speed to 190kt. They were then cleared down to 4,000ft and one minute later the controller cleared the flight for the ILS approach to runway 24L. On the approach, which was

stabilised, the weather deteriorated around the airfield, with lightning activity and downpours that restricted visibility. With an unexpected strong tail/crosswind the aircraft crossed the threshold about 40ft too high and touched down just under halfway down the 9,000ft wet runway, but was not able to stop before the end and overran at 80kt. It veered to the left, down a slope, ending up in a gulley. The aircraft caught fire, but everyone on board was evacuated safely.

The Air France A340 after overrunning the runway in Toronto. (Lee Thomas)

They anticipate other crew members' needs and carry out instructions as directed

Good teamwork is thinking ahead and being prepared for what other people might need so that you can react quickly to requests, particularly if the other person is under pressure. Also there are times when you just need to do as you're told. If you are supposed to carry out a task, or are asked to do something that may not be your job but you are capable of doing it and it seems reasonable, then just do it without question or complaint. I get concerned when I hear of co-pilots who have just done a CRM course going out of their way to question all the captain's decisions and constantly giving their opinions. They use the excuse that this is good CRM. It is not, it is being a pain in the neck. Similarly, if you are the captain and the monitoring pilot or PNF, and the first officer asks you to do something that is perfectly reasonable, then also just do it and don't pull rank.

They are open and honest about thoughts, concerns and intentions

Good leadership and teamworking is about letting others know what is in your mind and what your intentions are. Assuming people will figure out what you are going to do with scant clues is never useful, as is letting them know quite late of your change in plan. It is also about keeping others informed, where appropriate, about how you are feeling, so that they can work with you better. If you are not on the ball, or are particularly tired after a poor night's sleep followed by six sectors, then it may be worth letting the people you work with know. Otherwise they will be relying on someone who they assume is working at 100 per cent, and they don't need to find out you're not at the wrong time.

They give and receive criticism and praise well, and admit mistakes

It is almost impossible for an individual to develop their performance without any feedback: everyone needs to know where they stand and the effect of any changes they make. Self-assessment is all very well, but it is not as useful as feedback from others. Teams will struggle to develop unless they give each other feedback, and this means giving criticism and praise. However, unless it is done well it will have limited or even negative value. The trick to both giving and receiving criticism well is to have the right attitude towards it. Criticism, after all, is just information about you that other people have and you may not have. As all information is valuable and you are the most important person in the world, then information about you must therefore be priceless.

They confidently do and say what is important to them

Many a misunderstanding or confusion has occurred because people have not said or done things with confidence. If you are landing two thirds of the way down the runway you are not 'a little long', comments are not 'Mmmh...', and the advice is not 'Perhaps we might not make it.' The conversation in the

Erebus accident was full of uncertain expressions and hesitations, whereas what was required was, 'I am very concerned about our position and would like us to climb back to Safety Altitude.' If you say or do things without conviction, then others are not clear whether you are sure yourself or whether you really mean it, and will react accordingly. This however does not give you a licence to be stubborn or dogmatic; the ability to compromise is a key factor in effective teamwork.

Zürich

Flight 3597, an Avro 146, departed Berlin-Tegel for a flight to Zürich and climbed to a cruising altitude of FL270. It was cleared to descend down to FL160 as the crew were carrying out an approach briefing for a runway 14 ILS approach at Zürich. Having been further cleared down to FL130, the crew were told to prepare for a runway 28 VOR/DME approach. Another approach briefing was carried out and the minimum descent altitude was found to be 2,390ft. The aircraft was cleared for the runway 28 approach, descending to 4,000ft after which it turned right for the final approach. A preceding aircraft reported having the runway in sight at 2.2 DME and the captain reported reaching the minimum descent altitude and said that he could see the ground. A little later the radio altimeter reported 500ft AGL, followed by a 'minimum' warning. The captain then ordered a go-around, but this was too late. The aircraft struck trees and crashed. The treetops were at 1,784ft. The causes were found to be as follows:

- The accident is attributable to the fact that on the final approach, in own navigation, of the standard VOR/DME approach, the aircraft flew controlled into a wooded range of hills, because the flight crew deliberately continued the descent under instrument flight conditions below the minimum altitude for the approach without having the necessary prerequisites. The flight crew initiated the go-around too late.

- The commander deliberately descended below the minimum descent altitude of the standard VOR/DME approach 28 without having the required visual contact to the approach lights or the runway

- The co-pilot made no attempt to prevent the continuation of the flight below the minimum descent altitude.

CASE STUDY

The Crossair BAe146 at Zurich (Indo Richardt)

They demonstrate respect, empathy and tolerance for other people

Everyone is different. We have different values, beliefs and personalities. We like to do things differently, and we have different opinions about how things should be done. This is not because we like to be difficult, but because we all have different experiences, and we use those experiences to inform our actions. We also all have the ability to make mistakes. Furthermore although you may not necessarily be in agreement, demonstrating empathy is about showing that you understand their position and how they might be feeling. If you have difficulty with people having different views and doing things differently to you, or you are intolerant of other people getting something wrong or making the wrong judgement, then you will not be a great team player or leader.

They involve others in planning and share activities fairly, appropriate to abilities

If the people you work with are involved in the planning, they are more likely both to agree with what you are trying to do, and to have a clear understanding of how to do it, and can therefore think for themselves. Giving others all the boring jobs and keeping the interesting bits for yourself does not endear you to your fellow team members. In addition to the above you also get the benefit of using two brains rather than one, and getting a different perspective on things. Furthermore, if you are liable like me to forget things, then having someone else involved is always going to be useful.

Behaviour

A lot of what we describe as good leadership and teamwork is based on the way we behave, our verbal or non-verbal actions; and so it is perhaps relevant to explore this subject further at this stage. What we observe people doing and saying is how we describe their behaviour. This is our only reference as we cannot see inside someone else's mind. However, a person's behaviour – what they do and say – is often an expression of their attitude, as what we are thinking tends to come out in our actions. This is not always true, however, because sometimes we do things without thinking, particularly if we are not paying attention.

In fact there are several things that influence the way we behave, and they are the following:

- Your emotional state.
- Your mental capacity to think rationally (for you).
- Your level of alertness and energy.
- Your habits that could be strongly influenced by your culture.
- Your skill level in managing your behaviour.
- The environment and how you have perceived things.
- Your perception of what you see, feel and hear.
- Your willingness to take risk.

However, the main drivers of your behaviour towards other people, rather than things, is your attitude together with the possibility of gaining a benefit from a particular behaviour. All of these things are interconnected and affect each other. Rational thinking is based on your values, beliefs and perceptions that drive your thoughts and emotions, which in turn can influence your thoughts and further emotions. Your habits are developed from what you previously have thought and did on a regular basis, which would have given you an associated emotional anchoring experience. Habits are engaged depending on your level of alertness, which can be influenced by how important you consider the situation.

Your attitude is a collective term for your values and beliefs in respect of a person, thing, idea or situation. In simple terms it is what you think about someone or something. Values are your priorities or what is important to you. They could be considered as just more thoughts, but add a little more understanding to what attitude is and are thus included in the definition. Some attitudes are deep-rooted and based on considerable past experience and personal testing, although others are less firmly held and can often be changed by a simple bit of information.

People tend to communicate with each other in response to what they see and hear from the other person, and thus behaviour tends to breed behaviour. Another person's behaviour will influence a change in your behaviour, and this will vary in proportion to your level of expectation and its appropriateness. In other words, if someone behaves as you would expect and appropriately, this will not influence your behaviour very much, but if they behave unexpectedly and inappropriately, it is likely to cause a change in your behaviour. Developing this further; the way people behave towards you is often as a result of something you have said or done — or possibly omitted to do. This does not mean you have done anything wrong, but people will behave according to what they have perceived about you.

I believe behaviour is a choice, and because it is a choice then people are responsible for their behaviour. I also believe that personality and behaviour are in essence two sides of the same coin. Your behaviour is a demonstration of your personality, and as most people do not have the energy to put on an act for any length of time, then your behaviour is really who you are.

The premise that 'You can change your behaviour but not your personality', I therefore believe is not true. I think you can change your personality, because your personality is reflected in your behaviour and, as I have stated above, I think behaviour is a choice. But this is not something that will occur overnight and in fact may take many years. Nevertheless if you consistently and determinedly choose different behaviour, then over time your personality will change, as this becomes your natural state.

However, sometimes it does not feel as if it is a choice, particularly when you react instantaneously to something, which is a natural human reaction. The response to threat for instance is fight, flight or freeze. In these situations I think where the choice occurs is in the decision either to continue with the reaction or to adopt another behaviour. For example, if someone is abusive towards you, an immediate response would likely be that you are angry, but then within a second or so you have an opportunity to choose your ongoing behaviour, which may be to ignore the person or to allow yourself to continue to be angry and respond accordingly.

So in respect of our interaction with others – what makes us choose our behaviour? I think it is a combination of thoughts that you have about yourself and thoughts you have about the other person, linked with the benefits or damage that you think might accrue from behaving in a particular way. As the benefits or risks are dependent on your behaviour, what you are in essence choosing therefore is the thoughts you have – and it is these thoughts that drive your behaviour.

Choices of Behaviour

The good news, if you are interested in managing your behaviour, is that I believe there are principally only four choices of behaviour, because there are only four typical combinations of thoughts that you have. These choices are Direct Aggression, Indirect Aggression, Submissive and Assertive behaviour.

Directly aggressive behaviour

This is characterized by raising the voice, being abusive, abruptness, interrupting, invading space, glaring eye contact or eye contact that is just a second longer than it needs to be, gesticulating, finger pointing and generally crashing around.

This behaviour is driven by the thought that you are better than the other person, you are more senior and have more authority, you have more knowledge, more experience, your opinions are more valid – and of course you are right. They on the other hand are junior, inferior, insignificant, clearly wrong and annoying as well. What is most disturbing is that when we have these thoughts we give ourselves permission to behave aggressively. It is very difficult to rant and rave when you know you are wrong. But just having these thoughts is not enough for us to adopt this behaviour, we need to see a benefit in doing so.

The key benefits we think we get from choosing this behaviour is that we tend to get our way, get our point across, keep in control and save time. Unfortunately the long term effects on ourselves, the people around us and our work, are that we lose respect, are avoided, create fear, become stressed, are disliked and restrict creativity.

Indirectly aggressive behaviour

This is characterized by sarcasm, being two faced, spreading rumours, gossip and belittling remarks. It is being dishonest, lying, manipulation and ignoring others. It is often hidden behind humour or authority and is confusing for the person on the receiving end. A smile is not uncommon here.

This behaviour is driven by similar thoughts to those that drive direct aggression except the difference is that you won't tell the other person what those thoughts are. They may suspect, but of course when challenged you will dismiss them as being all in their imagination.

The key benefits we think we get from this behaviour is that we undermine others, get popularity and have a bit of fun. The long term effects are that we are not trusted, people tend to get revenge, and we become isolated.

Submissive behaviour

This is characterized by under confidence, avoidance of eye contact, reluctance to say anything, ask questions or make decisions, and certainly a difficulty to say no. Agreeing with everyone, trying to be liked and not expressing an opinion are also examples of submissive behaviour.

This behaviour is driven by the thought that you are a lesser being, are new, have little authority, do not have the experience or knowledge, and are most likely to be wrong. The other person seems to know what they are doing, looks more important, is more senior and generally right.

The key benefits we think we get from choosing this behaviour is that we have a quiet life, people will like us, we avoid confrontation and have no responsibility. The long term effects are that we feel resentful, do not get what we want, are ignored, overworked and lose self esteem.

Assertive behaviour

This behaviour is driven by the thoughts that you are comfortable with who you are, your opinions, values and beliefs, and doing things that are important to you. But you also respect other people, their opinions, values and beliefs, and doing things that are important to them. In other words it is a combination of self respect and respect for other people.

Assertive behaviour is characterized by friendliness, being open and honest, expressing feelings and opinions, calmness, confidence, listening to understand, compromise, questioning, saying no, asking for what you want or need, and demonstrating empathy. When we behave assertively we are also good at giving others criticism and praise, and likewise we are good at receiving it. Your eye contact and body language are comfortable and you often use humour in your conversation. It is the sort of behaviour you choose when in a social environment with close friends.

The benefits of choosing assertive behaviour is that we tend to get all the things that we think we get from the other choices but without the consequential effects.

Behaving assertively is fundamental to good airmanship.

How can we learn to behave assertively more often?

Firstly, we need to recognize that it is not easy, particularly in difficult situations. I think we can all behave assertively when things are going our way, or when we are with people we like and the job is getting done smoothly. But when the pressure is on, and people are not doing what you have asked; or you suspect they don't like you or respect you, which could be because you have made a mistake, then it is very easy to slip into aggressive or submissive behaviour.

I think this is mainly because unpleasant past experiences trigger negative thoughts that in turn trigger negative feelings. Once we have those feelings then it is very difficult to behave other than in accordance with those feelings, unless we employ a considerable amount of acting. Sadly, because we are not all great actors, other people tend to sense our true thoughts and feelings.

Secondly therefore, we need to identify what our triggers are so that we are not caught off guard and can manage our thoughts before it is too late.

Thirdly, we need to do a behavioural 'go-around' as one of my colleagues Sam Webb likes to call it. The process that triggers our thoughts, feelings and behaviour is based on emotive past experiences and is extremely rapid and powerful. Therefore initially we might not be able to prevent our reaction, but we can recognise what is happening with practice, take a deep breath and try and change our thoughts.

Lastly therefore, we must think positively about ourselves and positively about the other person. One way of doing this is to recognize that as a human being you have certain rights, which are principally the following:

- You have the right to be treated with respect.
- You have the right to express your opinion.
- You have the right to do things that are important to you.
- You have the right to ask for what you want.
- You have the right to make mistakes, be unaware or be unskilled.

Clearly, if we are prepared to take up these rights then we must be prepared to give these same rights to other people. When we either deny ourselves these rights or deny others these rights, then we are on our way to behaving inappropriately.

Throughout the above, we need to manage our body language, eye contact and tone so that they are consistent with our thoughts; otherwise others might perceive our behaviour incorrectly which might cause a negative reaction. Choosing the right thoughts and having good non-verbal skills completes the package that others will perceive.

In essence it all boils down to our attitude. Our attitude to life, to the people around us and to our approach to work, will be the dominant influence on our thoughts – and it is our thoughts that will drive our behaviour from one moment to the next.

CASE STUDY

Managlore

On the 22nd May 2010 an Air India Express Boeing 737 was approaching Managlore from Dubai. The captain had been asleep for 1hr 40 mins of the flight and in the descent, which was late, no approach briefing was recorded. The aircraft was high at all times on the profile and failed to intercept the glideslope correctly, which resulted in them being twice the normal height. The captain disconnected the autopilot and increased their rate of descent to 4,000ft/min, which triggered numerous GPWS warnings. Although the aircraft landed a long way down the runway, the captain selected reverse and then tried to go-around, but the aircraft overran and crashed into a gorge with the loss of 168 lives. Interestingly, the experienced co-pilot suggested a go-around 4 times, the last of which he actually transmitted on the radio – perhaps a call for help.

Air India Express B737 at Managlore

How to take control in a difficult situation

All the courses and all the books and all the advice say the same thing. Even though you are not the pilot flying or in command of the flight, you have a responsibility to yourself, your crew and your passengers to ensure the safety of the aircraft – and if that requires taking control then so be it.

In practice it is not so straightforward. Firstly, things generally happen far too quickly and your brain spools up far too slowly, hindered all the time by the thought 'this can't be happening'. Secondly, there are a number of factors at play, such as the culture of the organization, who the captain's friends are in management, what will happen if you over react and are wrong and many more. Finally, the other person's personality and their condition at the time might prevent you from being able to communicate with them. Sometimes they actually do not hear what you are saying because they have lost situation awareness, are disoriented or are simply choosing to ignore you.

Therefore, the following technique might help if you are ever in this awful situation, and you genuinely feel the safety of the aircraft is at risk.

Stay Assertive and manage your body language. What will help you to do this, is if you maintain positive thoughts, and have empathy and tolerance by remembering that:

They have the right to be treated with respect – and so do you.

They have the right do things that are important to them – and so do you.

They have the right to make mistakes – and so do you.

Then follow through this mnemonic – **SECAT**.

S tate factual observations and confirm intentions.
   'Captain we are 100ft high and have a 20kt tailwind, what are your intentions.'

E xpress concerns and make suggestions.
   'I am concerned with our approach and suggest we reduce speed.'

C hallenge
   'Captain, why are you continuing?' Listen and be willing to compromise.

A sk for what you want and explain consequences.
   'Captain, I would like you to go-around or else we might overrun.'

T ake control
   State firmly *'GO-AROUND'* at the right time, and then if necessary *'I have control'* and take control.

CASE STUDY

Flash Airlines

On the 3rd January 2004 a Boeing 737 from the Egyptian charter company Flash Airlines took from Sharm-el-Sheikh at night and entered a right turn. Even though the co-pilot repeatedly warned of overbank, the aircraft continued to bank and flew into the sea with the loss of 148 lives.

Wreckage from the Flash B737 in the Red Sea

Leadership

I think leadership is nearly as slippery a fish as airmanship or seamanship, and it suffers from the same mantra – 'I know what it is but I just can't define it'. Possibly one of the reasons why this may be the case is that they are almost one and the same thing. What I mean by this is that a lot of the characteristics of good leadership are the same as those of airmanship, as described above. Having sound technical knowledge, skills and attitudes, sound operational knowledge, skills and attitudes, and sound non-technical knowledge, skills and attitudes are the traits of a good leader. Good leaders demonstrate the non-technical performance indicators routinely, not just once in a while, and they are respected for these reasons. They communicate well, they are good at teamworking, they manage their workload, they know what is going on around them, they plan ahead, and they solve problems and make decisions. However, I think there are five additional things that distinguish leadership from airmanship or good management, and these are having vision, drive, independence, integrity and courage.

Having vision

Leaders tend to have vision. They know what they want to achieve and they are also often clear about how to get there. They see the big picture and they are easily able to prioritise things in order to achieve their vision. They often appear to be very decisive and to take the initiative, but this is just because they are clear about what needs to be done.

Having drive and resilience

Leaders tend to have drive. They get up and go, and keep going until they have achieved what they want. They may change the plan, take a step backwards or have a break, but they rarely give up.

Having independence

Leaders have a sense of independence. They do not need others to think for them or give them direction, which is why they can sometimes make poor decisions. Nevertheless it is a key trait. They can do things without seeking the approval of others and if they fail they are not concerned with what others think. They find their own resources and plough their own furrow, and at times it might mean that they have to break the rules.

Having integrity

Leaders are true to their beliefs. They do what they say they are going to do. They don't waver in the wind or follow the crowd. They are honest with themselves, and they are very clear about what is right and what is wrong. And they do the right thing.

Having courage

Leaders do have courage. They have the courage of their convictions. They take risks when they need to and when it is appropriate. They do not allow their fears to stop them doings things that they know they should do. They don't hide behind others and they don't avoid conflict.

The importance of leadership

Is it important to have a good leader to achieve a task successfully? This question has created much discussion and split opinion into two camps. Some believe that leadership is essential for a team to be effective, while others believe that although there should be a leader in any team, it is not the most essential ingredient for that team to be effective. I believe both camps are right, but in different situations. I think leadership is essential if the team is a rabble – disorganised, unclear of their objectives, with ambiguous roles and responsibilities, in conflict and having inertia. An autocratic leader will soon put everyone in line, give them direction, tell each person what they are supposed to do and make key decisions. The team will become much more effective.

Concorde – leadership epitomised. (Harm Rutten)

However, if members of the team have good teamworking skills, are clear on what they are trying to achieve, have clear roles and responsibilities, communicate well and are able to make their own decisions, then the importance of leadership is far less. Yes, a leader is needed as a representative for third parties, to co-ordinate discussion and to make final decisions, but the team generally will function pretty well on its own. In fact, the arrival of an autocratic leader in this situation will severely damage the effectiveness of the team. On a modern flight deck I would hope that the latter situation would prevail, and therefore a modicum of leadership, together with good teamwork and a great deal of airmanship, should suffice for most aircraft commanders.

Teamworking

Some people have strong experiences to support the theory that the best way to get anything done is to have a knowledgeable and decisive leader who just tells others what to do; and they then do it. Better still, if they want something done properly, then it's best to do it themselves. They think team-working just gets in the way of efficiency, wastes time and can dangerously undermine the confidence and momentum of the leader's decision. Compromise by definition cannot be the best solution. 'Black' maybe the best course of action, or 'white' – but never 'grey'.

However, when achieving a task people undertake three major activities. Firstly they decide what they are going to do, then they plan how they are going to do it, and then they do it. In my experience, a single person can make the majority of the decisions that are required in the first two activities, but when it comes to implementation and they need the help of others, then the task is more successful when people agree with what they are doing and are clear about the plan. This is often only achieved when everyone in the team is involved in all those decisions.

One person telling others what to do and them then doing it is not neces-sarily teamworking. A fundamental feature of teamworking is that members of the team are part of the decision making process, not only in the planning stages but also in the implementation. This is critical because the plan rarely runs as advertised, and team members need to be able to think on their feet and make decisions appropriately. This does not mean decision making by committee, it just means that all team members are involved in the process, so that they have the opportunity to have an input, and better understand the decision that is made.

On the flight deck I am a firm advocate of the captain's authority. He or she is ultimately responsible for the safe conduct of the flight and therefore is entitled to make the final decision. I would go even further in that I fully support the need for captains to make unilateral decisions if the circum-stances (usually shortage of time) require this is to be done.

I do not believe that team-building by working on the team as a whole is so effective. Forcing groups of people to develop as a team by using unnatu-ral interventions can have the opposite effect and the team is irreparably damaged. I prefer to develop individuals to become good team members and then give opportunities for the team to progress in a natural manner. This has the added benefit of ensuring that when individuals leave the team and join another, then the work is not lost.

In aviation this is particularly relevant because teams come together for short periods of time and the opportunity for teams to develop into effective units is not available. Hence the preponderance of SOPs and prescriptive training, which are designed to minimise the threat of an ineffective team. There are many theories around on the make-up of a team that are all perfectly valid and make a lot of sense, but which I think are only practical if everything else is in place. We don't have the luxury of selection, so we are normally lumbered with the people we have, and given the choice I would always take a team of similar individuals who are good team members rather than a collection of different people who cannot function.

WORKLOAD MANAGEMENT

The workload management performance indicators

Managing workload and maintaining capacity are the biggest challenges a pilot faces. Capacity is the thinking reserve you have available to you. Once this has run out and your brain is full of information, emotion, pending decisions, and confusion, it ceases to operate and shuts down. Therefore managing your workload effectively protects this precious reserve, because you can't do it retrospectively. In other words when you are in the swamp and are running out of capacity, you do not have enough left to sort the situation out and plan ahead. Captain Colin Budenberg of Thomsonfly uses a brilliant expression which gives pilots a perfect understanding of their role in this respect, and that is 'You are paid to be comfortable'. Thinking about all the things you might need to do in order to meet this requirement will usually result in your workload management and situation awareness being at a high standard. I think for most people, if not everyone, we don't hear things, see things or feel things when we are intensely concentrating on something else, and several accidents have shown that this has been a factor.

Crew members are calm, relaxed, careful, not impulsive and consider the implications of their actions.

The ability to be calm under pressure means that the brain is performing at its best and does more thinking. Being relaxed means that the body is going to do things you want it to do, rather than being uncoordinated and making mistakes. Furthermore, remaining calm also does not distract others; it gives confidence and it allows them to work at full capacity. During the Qantas A380 incident Captain Richard De Crespigny said there was no panic on the flight deck and that he felt that he consciously tried to remain calm. He explained that remaining calm was about controlling your breathing –

breathe in 2 seconds, wait 2 seconds then breathe out, a technique that might be useful to learn, as it seems to work! In high workload situations it is tempting to make quick decisions because it gets them out the way, but it is essential to be careful and not to rush into decisions or actions that might cause additional problems later on. Also, a good habit to get into before taking any action is think about the implications of doing so. Simply ask, if I do this – what might happen?

Dubrovnik

On the 3rd April 1996 a USAF CT-43 crashed into hills at 2,300ft while making an NDB approach to Dubrovnik in Croatia. During mission planning the crew failed to note that the Dubrovnik approach required two automatic direction finders; the CT-43 had only one. An error in planning the route added 15 minutes to the planned flight time and may have caused the crew to rush the approach. According to the report, the pilots did not properly configure the aircraft for landing before starting the final approach. They came in 80kt above final approach speed, without clearance from the tower. The rushed approach, late configuration and a radio call from a pilot on the ground may have distracted the crew from adequately monitoring the final approach, which proved to be 9° left of the correct course.

The USAF CT-43 in the hills north of Dubrovnik

CASE STUDY

They prepare, prioritise and schedule tasks effectively

Workload management starts with good preparation, setting priorities and making sure you do things in the most effective order. You cannot start more than one task at the same time, so whatever you are doing there will be a schedule of activities. I do not think you can prepare too much: life rarely allows the luxury of time. This does not mean procrastination, because that is in the domain of decision making, which will be explained later. Planning is the first part of the process of implementing a decision, and you can be as thorough as you like. It will always pay off.

CASE STUDY

Cali

On the 20th December 1995 American Airlines Boeing 757 N651AA took off from Miami to Cali, Colombia. While descending to FL200, Cali control cleared the flight for a direct Cali VOR approach and report at Tulua VOR, followed one minute later by a clearance for a straight-in VOR DME Rozo 1 approach to runway 19, which was unexpected but welcomed as it saved

The American Airlines 757 N651AA at Mexico City. (Robert Campbell)

time which they had lost. The crew then went to select the Rozo NDB on the FMC, by inserting 'R' as per the approach plates' code for Rozo. But 'R' in the FMC database brought up Romeo, a NDB 150nm from Rozo, and as it was first on the list they selected it and executed the command. The aircraft had just passed Tulua VOR when it started a turn to the left towards Romeo. The crew did not notice this turn immediately but then were confused as they were expecting a straight-in approach. Whilst they were turning back towards Cali the GPWS warning sounded. The crew tried to climb with increased engine power and the nose up, but the spoilers were still deployed from the descent. The stick shaker then activated and the aircraft crashed into a mountain at about 8,900ft.

The probable causes of this accident were:

- The flight crew's failure to adequately plan and execute the approach and their inadequate use of automation.

- Failure of the flight crew to discontinue the approach into Cali, despite numerous cues alerting them of the inadvisability of continuing the approach.

- The lack of situational awareness of the flight crew regarding vertical navigation, proximity to terrain, and the relative location of critical radio aids.

- Failure of the flight crew to revert to basic radio navigation at the time when the FMS-assisted navigation became confusing and demanded an excessive workload in a critical phase of the flight.

Contributing to the cause of the accident were:

- The flight crew's ongoing efforts to expedite their approach and landing in order to avoid potential delays.

- The flight crew's execution of the GPWS escape manoeuvre while the speed brakes remained deployed.

They manage time efficiently when carrying out tasks

Tracking time, making sure you don't drift along unnecessarily or spend too much time on things that are not important, will help you to preserve this most essential resource. Using routines and checklists to do things quickly, as well as simple tools, all help, but what really makes a difference is constantly trying to get faster at regular tasks, by identifying how they can be done better.

They offer and accept assistance, delegate if necessary and call for help early

If you have spare capacity, then offer it to others. If you don't have spare capacity then delegate or ask for help, but do it early or you won't have the capacity to ask when you really need it. This is an attitude thing. We either don't want to interfere or resent others interfering with us, and we like to keep control of our tasks. It takes a lot of trust to delegate responsibility to someone else and allow them to get on with it, or even admit that they probably can do a better job than you.

CASE STUDY

Bahrain

On the 23rd August 2000 a Gulf Air Airbus A320 flown by the captain was conducting a night approach to Bahrain International Airport. He disconnected the auto pilot/flight director when visual with the runway, but then, approximately 1nm from touchdown at about 600ft and at an airspeed of 185kt, requested a left hand orbit because they were too high and fast on the approach. During the tight left-hand turn the flaps were fully extended and the landing checklist completed. When the aircraft crossed the extended runway centreline the crew reported they wanted to abort the landing. A controller gave them clearance to climb to 2,500ft onto a 300° heading to prepare for another approach. The plane's speed began increasing to 185kt as it began to climb to 1,000ft in a 5° nose-up attitude. During the go-around at approximately 1,000ft, the aircraft entered a rapid descent, 15° nose down. As the GPWS sounded, the captain ordered the flaps to be raised and moved the side stick aft. The aircraft impacted the sea at a 6.5° nose-down angle at about 280kt.

The investigation showed that the accident was the result of a fatal combination of many contributory factors, both at the individual and systemic levels. The individual factors particularly during the approach and final phases of the flight were:

- The captain did not adhere to a number of SOPs, such as: significantly higher than standard aircraft speeds during the descent and the first approach; not stabilising the approach on the correct approach path; performing an orbit, a non-standard manoeuvre, close to the runway at low altitude; and not performing the correct go-around procedure.

- In spite of a number of deviations from the standard flight parameters and profile, the first officer (PNF) did not call them out, or draw the attention of the captain to them, as required by SOPs.

- A perceptual study indicated that during the go-around after the orbit, it appears that the flight crew may have experienced spatial disorientation, which could have caused the captain to perceive (falsely) that the aircraft was 'pitching up'. He responded by making a 'nose down' input, and as a result the aircraft descended and flew into the shallow sea.

- Neither the captain nor the first officer perceived, or effectively responded to, the threat of increasing proximity to the ground, in spite of repeated GPWS warnings.

The Gulf Air A320 being retrieved from the sea (Bahrain CAA)

They monitor, cross-check, and review actions conscientiously

Constantly checking if you are on track, monitoring what is going on and cross-checking, double-checking and even triple-checking will ensure that the task stays in control and doesn't get away from you. Gross error checks are not a nicety, they are an essential. Try to guess what V1, VR and V2 are before the computer or manual tells you, and try to estimate what the remaining fuel will be halfway through the flight. When you get in the habit of doing these sorts of things you will get caught out less often.

CASE STUDY

Auckland

On the 12th March 2003 a Singapore Airlines Boeing 747 started its take-off from Auckland International Airport for Singapore with almost a full load of passengers. When the captain rotated the aeroplane for lift-off the tail struck the runway and scraped for some 500m until the aeroplane became airborne. The incident occurred because the rotation speed was 33kt less than the 163kt required for the aeroplane weight. A take-off weight transcription error led to the miscalculation of the take-off data, which resulted in a low thrust setting and the excessively slow take-off reference speeds. During the take-off the aeroplane moved close to the runway edge and the pilots did not respond correctly to a stall warning. Had it left the runway or stalled, a more serious accident could have occurred.

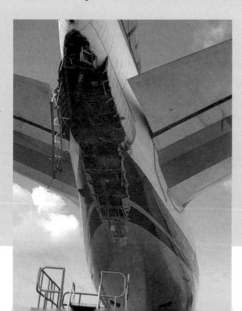

The tail plane of the Singapore Airlines 747 at Auckland after the tail scrape (Chris Norton)

They follow procedures appropriately and consistently

Procedures have been developed to reflect best practice, so use this resource whenever you can. They have also been developed from the experience of others and by taking into account situations that you may not be aware of, particularly if someone has been caught out. They are generally presented in an order that has been well thought out and discussed, and which is mindful of the implications of each step on other systems and processes. However, if you genuinely believe that the circumstances dictate that the procedure is not appropriate, then you should act accordingly.

CASE STUDY

Lexington

On the 27th August 2006 a Comair CRJ taxied out from Lexington airport for an early morning flight. During start-up and taxi the crew typically discussed social and career issues. There was little other traffic and one controller on duty. Weather at Lexington was fine on the morning with a small shower approaching from the west. It was still dark just after 06:00 as the CRJ taxied out for take-off. The crew were cleared for a runway 22 departure, which is Lexington's main runway. Because the runway had been repaved recently with an added safety area at the approach end of runway 22, one taxiway was no longer in use; also the taxi route to runway 22 had been changed. The crew lined up on the shorter, 3,500ft and unlit runway 26 and although one of the pilots made a remark about the lack of runway light illumination, the take-off was continued. The fully laden CRJ was not able to rotate within the runway distance and continued past the runway end where it struck several trees and burst into flames.

The Comair CRJ at Lexington. (NTSB

They concentrate on one thing at a time and ensure tasks are complete

Make sure you concentrate on one thing at time, complete what you plan to do and do not allow yourself to be distracted. This might mean employing assertive behaviour and asking others to give you time, but if you must be distracted make sure you mark where you are in the task, so that you can continue what you were doing. Remember, distraction is a mental process. A person can concentrate quite well even when there is lot of noise and movement, as proven by Formula 1 drivers; but as soon as the mind begins to wander then very little of what is happening around you is noticed, irrespective of how quiet it may be.

They manage interruptions, distractions, variations and failures effectively

Pilots will always be distracted and interrupted when flying – it is the nature of the job. The skill is to manage these well, which means where possible not allowing yourself to be interrupted. However, if you are distracted make sure you can get back to where you were in the previous task, without forgetting something. Informal techniques such as placing unusual objects in weird places are good ways to remind yourself to do something. As for failures, an instructor once told me – 'An emergency is only a malfunction that is badly handled'. This is great advice, which of course I was never able to follow and always ended up making things worse, due to a combination of panic, making assumptions and a desire for the problem to go away quickly.

How to manage your workload

Workload management is an essential skill of airmanship. The ability to know what needs to be done, to prioritise tasks and to ensure they are carried out efficiently using the resources available to you is fundamental to safe and successful operations. Sometimes I feel like the ball in a pinball machine. I allow my environment and the people around me to dictate what I do and when. I bounce from one activity to another, I sometimes get stuck in a corner doing nothing and then I am hurled back into the melee with not a clue as to what will happen next. Apart from being great fun, it generally achieves little. For the average person, cooking, car maintenance and DIY are good examples of non-aviation situations where a high level of workload management is required, so perhaps we can use these opportunities to practice our workload management skills. To manage our workload better it might be helpful to consider the following process:

First. We need to plan and prepare what we are going to do. Some old axioms can remind us of this, like the six Ps – prior preparation and planning prevents poor performance – or the one I prefer: Fail to prepare, prepare to fail. So we need to develop the schedule of what we are going to do, and the following questions will help us:

– What is important? What is urgent?
– What will get worse if it is ignored?
– What needs other things to be done first? What can be started and left to develop? What is the logical sequence of tasks?

Second. Once we have our tasks organised in order, we can then prepare the tools and resources that we need to carry out the tasks. Included in this are sub-routines that we may have developed, and ensuring that everything is positioned in the most accessible place. We might also need to learn things by heart, so that we can seamlessly continue through the task without stopping to refer, which may not be possible if we have our hands full.

Third. We begin the task whilst constantly monitoring what is happening, always double-checking where it is critical, and when something goes amiss putting a hold on activity until we are clear what to do next and have re-planned. A good technique to manage activities was told to me by Captain Emilios Economides, an ex Olympic sailor who used this during races. Focus your activities on definitive time windows and concentrate planning on the next time window. So during taxiing, review the take-off and initial climb, then during the climb review the transition to the cruise, and so on. This way you are always ahead of the game, but are not overloaded with too much information.

Fourth. During the planning phase and the task itself make use of alarms, triggers, colours and notes to keep track of what is going on. If necessary, record activities so that you don't have to rely on your memory. Use your own techniques, personal checklists and mantras to keep on top of things. Finally when you are finished, tidy up loose ends, do the paperwork and reset things that you know you will need next time.

Sea Harrier – there aren't many higher workloads. (Keith Campbell)

SITUATION AWARENESS

What is situation awareness?

It is as old as the hills. I remember chatting to an old pilot who used to fly Constellations and DC-8s in the 1950s and 1960s. He related his first diversion landing into Beirut on a very dark night as a first officer. He had lost the plot but fortunately the more experienced captain knew what he was doing. The next morning he was shocked to see a large hill close to the airfield – he really had no idea it was there. In fact the thought occurred to him that he could easily have done a visual circuit straight into that hill. Then he said casually, 'Boy, in those days you had to keep an eye on everything going on around you and think ahead at all times.' That will do for me as a definition of situation awareness:

'Knowing what is going on around you and being prepared for what might happen.'

It is a skill that can be developed and requires people to understand what is happening around them, so that they not only monitor and keep track of what should be happening, but are also able to identify any threats to the safe and efficient progress of the operation. Although there is a lot to keep an eye on, and it requires a bit of skill, in principle situation awareness is really quite simple. Just monitor what's going on, understand what is happening, think ahead to what is likely to happen, anticipate and prepare accordingly. There are six main areas of which pilots need to be situationally aware: Systems, Task, Environment, Aircraft position, People, Time.

Why is situation awareness lost?

I think there are three direct causes for loss of situation awareness:

Reaching capacity

As already stated the brain has limited capacity – a finite ability to manage several tasks at the same time and process information. When this capacity is reached, a situation that can only be described as seizure takes place; in fact the brain does not even have any resource left to reboot. It is not a comfortable experience. You are not able to think or to grasp any information that you receive, and even simple things are beyond you. People around you are carrying on as normal and appear quite relaxed. They look at you with doubt and sympathy, and have a look in their eyes that says, 'How thick can you be?' similar in many ways to when you are extremely inebriated and everyone else is stone cold sober. Because life is dynamic, things are changing constantly, so when you have reached capacity you are not able to track or to comprehend what is happening around you, let alone be able to think ahead and plan. Thus situation awareness quickly breaks down.

Being 'switched off'

Occasionally referred to as 'mind in neutral', this of course is the opposite situation and occurs when you are in the land of the fairies. You appear to be operating but in fact your brain has shut down. Expressions such as 'the lights are on but nobody is in' and 'out to lunch' are apt descriptions. I think it is caused by either unintentional meditation or when you allow your mind to daydream and think of other things. Clearly the chances of maintaining situation awareness in this state are slim. Having a quiet nap is of course the ultimate example, but make sure you are wearing sunglasses so no-one notices.

Misperception

The final reason why situation awareness is lost is when you misinterpret what you see, hear or feel. There are many optical illusions in the world, some of which we are aware of but many of which we are not. Even when we know something is an optical illusion we still can't believe it, and I recommend Edward H. Adelson's work for evidence. Furthermore, if we are concentrating too deeply on one thing it is very easy to completely miss other things that are happening. Why we misinterpret things is difficult to explain. One obvious cause is that we have preconceptions and see or hear what we want to see or hear, but why we see things that are different to reality is a bit of a mystery because cameras do not have the same problem.

How to recognise loss of situation awareness?

Here are a few indicators that might mean a person has lost situation awareness, in relation to the above causes.

Reaching capacity	Being 'switched off'	Misperception
● Rapid eye movement. ● Mumbling. ● Contradicting themselves. ● Hyperactivity. ● Anxiousness. ● Glaring. ● 'Goldfish' look.	● Non-responsive. ● Inactivity. ● Staring at space.	● Saying or doing the wrong thing. ● Overconfidence.

What you should do when you have lost it

1. Recognise the fact and let relevant people know as soon as possible.

2. Stop what you are doing but don't allow yourself to wallow in a confused state. This does two things: first, it releases capacity; and second, it prevents you stumbling into an unknown situation. If you can hand over control then great, otherwise consider briefly letting go of the controls if possible or hold them in a neutral position.

3. Dismiss stressors. Often what is contributing to your loss of situation awareness is stress, such as being late and rushing, or trying to do too many things. Re-prioritise. Tell yourself that you will just have to be late or the passengers will just have to be disappointed, or you will not be able to achieve your ATC clearance. Safety is much more important at this point.

4. Contain the situation so that the problem does not get worse. This might mean level the wings and set a sensible attitude and power setting. Maintain height and possibly orbit, or climb to a safe altitude. Hand over control if appropriate – and almost always engage the autopilot.

5. Slowly start regaining situation awareness, which means taking things one step at a time. At each step verify that the information is correct. For instance, check your airspeed and verify that it is consistent with your attitude and power setting. Check your height and cross-check with standby instruments and QNH setting. Then start confirming your position, again cross-checking with whatever aids you have available. Use the resources that will help you.

6. Do not make any decisions until your situation awareness has fully returned.

7. Before doing anything, think ahead, anticipate and plan, so that you are not immediately back where you were, having lost situation awareness again.

How do you maintain it?

When you have situation awareness then you know what is going on around you. If you want to maintain it, then keep your mental 'APU' running continuously:

Anticipate
Think ahead, and use your imagination and experience to identify what might happen in the near future. Expect the unexpected.

Prepare
Do something about it if possible. Obviously you can't be prepared for everything, but there are simple and easy things you can do to make sure you are not caught out, or have to manage several things at once. Have Plans B, C and D ready if necessary.

Update
Continuously update your situation awareness. Track and monitor all the things you need to be aware of, and the progress of any activity.

The following table lists the areas that crews should be monitoring as required, which does not mean constantly, but they should have an idea of the status or condition of each of these elements at all times. Although there are a lot of items listed, not being aware of what is happening in any one might be distracting, or the start of an error chain.

The situation awareness performance indicators

Crew members are aware of what the aircraft and its systems are doing

As described above, there are a lot of things that you should be aware of at all stages of flight. Most of them don't require close monitoring because they don't change, but anything that is important and dynamic must be monitored.

CASE STUDY

Air France AF447

On the morning of the 1st June 2009 Air France Flight AF447, an Airbus A330, from Rio de Janeiro en route to Paris was passing through an area of tropical thunderstorms at 35,000ft. It is likely that icing caused the loss of airspeed indications and for the autopilot to disengage. The co-pilot who was the pilot flying whilst the captain had taken a rest, pitched up to almost 16° and the aircraft climbed to nearly 38,000ft, which caused the aircraft to stall. Despite the application of full power and intermittent

Air France Airbus A330 AF447 tailplane

Systems	Task	Environment	Aircraft Position	People	Time
Engines	Commercial	Weather system	Diversions	Flight crew	Endurance
APU	ATC	Runway condition	Other aircraft	Cabin crew	Slot times
Flying controls	Clearances	Precipitation	Height	Passengers	Time zones
Autopilot	Navigation	Cloud	Speed	Engineering	Local / GMT
FMS	Procedures	Forecasts	Direction	Dispatch	Circadian
Nav Aids	Checklists	Turbulence	Acceleration	Refuelling	Planning
Flight instruments	Start	Lightning	Location	Loadmasters	FTL
Alarms	Take-off	Icing	Attitude	Ramp handling	
Fuel	Climb	Wind	Ground vehicles	ATC	
Pressurisation	Descent	Wind shear	Buildings	Security	
Trim	Cruise	Visibility	Equipment	De-icing	
Wheels	Hold	Glare	Taxiways	Cleaning	
Brakes	Approach	Temperature	Runways	Catering	
Flaps and slats	Landing	Pressure	Energy	General public	
Radio	Go-around	Terrain		Knowledge	
Cabin atmosphere	Diversion	Habitation		Skills	
Fire	Taxi	Noise		Attitude	
Electrics	Weight	Birds		Fatigue	
Hydraulics	Parking	FOD		Hunger	
Bleed air	Passenger loading	Wake turbulence		Thirst	
Refuelling	Cargo	Political		Motivation	
Alarms	Security	Commercial		Health	
Anti-icing	Cabin service	Legal		Bladder state	
Heating	Cabin security	Security		Fitness (incl drugs/ alcohol)	
Pneumatics	Legalities			Awareness	
Doors	Documentation			Disorientation	
Lighting				Mental state	
IFE				Relationships	
Cargo bays				Culture	
Misc				Language	

changes in pitch, the aircraft remained in a stalled condition with the co-pilot maintaining predominantly pitch up command on the sidestick. The captain was called back and entered the flight deck to be confronted with an unusual situation, and comments from the two co-pilots that they did not know what was happening and had lost control of the aircraft. Although control between the pilots changed twice, and the airspeed indications returned, the aircraft remained in a pitched up attitude with an AoA of 30–40° and a sink rate of over 10,000ft/min, until it hit the sea with the loss of 228 lives. The interim report established that the crew did not comment on the almost continuous stall warning or recognize they were in a stall, even though they had an extremely high rate of descent, low airspeed, high pitch angle, unresponsive controls and buffet.

They are aware of where the aircraft is and its environment
It is very easy to get lost but this only becomes a problem if you run out of fuel, enter bad weather or hit something hard. Therefore, ensuring you know where your aircraft is in relation to its environment is one of the essentials of good airmanship.

Air China 747

On the 15th April 2002 an Air China Boeing B747 from Beijing were informed in the descent to Busan of a late runway change which required them to conduct a circling approach, of which they were not familiar. Having lost sight of the airfield and communications with ATC, the crew became lost and crashed into high ground 5 km from the runway, with the loss of 159 lives. The report found that the crew exercised poor CRM and lost situation awareness. They also did not brief for a missed approach, which they should have executed when they lost sight of the runway.

The Air China B747 at Busan

They are aware of the condition of the people involved in the operation, including passengers

Particularly in general aviation or executive jet operations, passengers have a major influence on the safe outcome of a flight. If passengers are in a hurry or aggressive, then expect to be pestered on any delays and be pressurised into continuing into bad weather. They do not have the same self-preservation systems as you do because they have watched too many happy-ending films and are unaware of the dangers. Furthermore, ground crew or passengers who have lost their own situation awareness and are overawed by what is happening are likely to do silly things such as walk into the tail rotor or engine intake.

They keep track of time and fuel

Although a technical activity, the process of monitoring fuel is important. The Portland accident is a classic example of losing fuel situation awareness. There have been countless incidents and accidents, particularly in general aviation, where pilots have not recognised the effects of the conditions on fuel management. Headwinds, lower flight levels, anti-icing systems, unusual configuration situations and avoidance of weather all create additional fuel burn. In addition, cross-feeding errors, fuel pump failures and fuel leaks have all conspired to cause aircraft to run out of fuel, or at least be a little embarrassed. The only solution is to monitor fuel used, fuel flow, fuel remaining and conditions ahead monotonously.

CASE STUDY

Vienna

On the 12th July 2000 Flight 3378 departed Crete for a flight to Hanover. The crew encountered problems fully raising the right-hand main landing gear, but it was decided to continue flight with the gear down and to divert to Munich. During the flight the calculated spare fuel at Munich decreased on the FMS. The crew now decided to divert to Vienna Airport instead. Approaching Vienna it appeared that there was not enough fuel on board. At about 12nm short of the runway, and at about 4,000ft altitude both engines quit. The crew were able to restart one engine for a short period of time, managing to reach the airport, but the aircraft landed in the grass some 500m from the runway 34 threshold. The left main gear broke off and the No.1 engine and wing sustained substantial damage as the aircraft slid for 600m before coming to rest.

Hapag Lloyd after gliding slightly unsuccessfully into Vienna. (Marcus Weigand)

They recognise what is likely to happen, plan, make pre-decisions and stay ahead of the situation

Just monitoring what is happening is pointless if you don't use the information. Constantly think ahead and project into the future what is currently happening. If you are en-route to Heathrow and the ATIS tells you there are severe thunderstorms in the South East of England, then you can guarantee you will have to hold for longer than normal, as the London area controllers will be manoeuvring aircraft all over the place. If you are also low on fuel, then start thinking about what you might be faced with. Start preparing for possibilities. This doesn't cost anything except a bit of effort, but it will avoid everything being done in a rush and mistakes made.

The importance of making pre-decisions is solely to release capacity at a critical time. Because the brain cannot process more that one problem at a time, if you have already made one of the decisions then you can concentrate on the next one. The most common example of a pre-decision is the 'Go/No Go' decision that is made should an engine failure occur at V1. Most pilots are familiar with this and can make the decision fairly calmly. Another example of a pre-decision that has been formalised by most operators is a mandatory go-around if not stabilised by key gates on the approach.

Taipei

On the 31st October 2000 a Singapore Airlines Boeing 747 taxied out for a runway 05L departure because runway 05R was closed for construction work. After reaching the end of taxiway NP, which ran parallel to the runway, the crew turned right into taxiway N1 and immediately made a 180° turn to runway 05R. After an approximately 6 second hold, they started their take-off roll. Weather conditions were very poor because of a typhoon in the area. On take-off, 3.5 seconds after V1, the aircraft hit concrete barriers, excavators and other equipment on the runway. The crew were aware of the fact that a portion of runway 05R was closed, and that runway 05R was only available for taxi. The flight crew did not review the taxi route in a manner sufficient to ensure they all understood that the route to runway 05L included the need for the aircraft to pass runway 05R, before taxiing onto runway 05L. The crew had the airport charts available when taxiing from the parking bay to the departure runway;

CASE STUDY

however, when the aircraft was turning from taxiway NP to taxiway NI and continued turning onto runway 05R, none of the flight crewmembers verified the taxi route. Further, none of the flight crewmembers confirmed orally which runway they had entered.

The Singapore Airlines B747 after hitting construction vehicles on take off at Taipei (Yao Zulin)

They identify threats to the safety of the aircraft and people, and take appropriate action

Similar to the performance indicator above, but this is a more formal process and might even require a formal question, such as 'What are the threats and what is going to cause problems?' Think what the conditions are and what is happening in the task. Be imaginative in identifying what can go wrong and what could cause that to happen. This is not about being pessimistic, this is about being realistic. Remember Murphy's Law: Whatever can go wrong, will go wrong. Just make sure it doesn't happen on your watch, or if it does, then you are prepared to deal with it. Finally, think about the actions you can take to avoid the threats, or what you might consider if the threats appear, and be prepared to trap any errors.

PROBLEM SOLVING

The problem solving performance indicators

Crew members identify and verify why things have gone wrong, and do not jump to conclusions or make uninformed assumptions

The first step in problem solving is to identify exactly what the problem is, and not to jump to conclusions and then take rushed actions. Sit on your hands or count to ten is good advice. Make sure that the aircraft is in a safe state. Remember: 'aviate, navigate, communicate' is the golden rule for managing most emergencies or problems.

Aviate

Ensure the aircraft is under control and will remain so for a reasonable time while you sort out the problem. Use the autopilot and other crew members to monitor the flight. An experienced captain and a junior co-pilot are equally good at flying an aircraft in a straight line at a safe altitude, but the captain is better placed to think through an unusual situation, so let the co-pilot fly the aircraft. This was well demonstrated by Captain Peter Burkill, who displayed exceptional airmanship in allowing his co-pilot to successfully land a powerless Boeing 777, with no casualties at all as described earlier.

Navigate

Ensure you are not going to hit anything, get lost, run out of fuel or go too far from a suitable landing area while you deal with the problem.

Communicate

Tell everyone who needs to know what your problem is, so that they can help you as best they can. This includes cabin crew, ATC, base maintenance, other aircraft and even passengers.

They seek accurate and adequate information from appropriate resources

There are numerous sources of information available to most pilots that you can use, ranging from the obvious engine instruments to the more bizarre. While flying helicopters I often used to note which direction the birds were landing or taking off, if I had no other indicators of where the wind was blowing. Take a note of smoke on the ground or wind streaks on the sea if you are expecting wind shear on the approach. With emergencies, make sure you look at all available indicators and cross-check the information wherever you can. In the Kegworth accident all the information the crew needed was available to them. The engine instruments, the vibration indicators and the manuals would have told them which engine had failed. Furthermore the passengers and cabin crew had first-hand information about what was happening, and the flight crew had the time to tap into all these resources.

They persevere working through a problem
Don't give up on a problem. This is the easiest thing to do when you don't understand what is happening and nothing makes sense. Just work it through and don't waste precious mental time and energy thinking it can't be done. Meticulously make notes if you can, so that you are not going over things again. Grind it out.

A problem solving process

Any mental process requires the use of questions to best manage the information that you have. The following questions are effective when dealing with a problem which can be defined by 'something that has gone wrong':

What should be happening? What is actually happening? Do we know why? What is the cause?

Then ask the same questions again on the next level down until you get to the root cause of the problem. In other words, find out what is the cause of the cause.

If you are struggling to find any cause, then analyse why it is this problem and not some other problem, why it is happening here and not there, at this time and not at other times, or with this person and not with other people.

See what is different between what, where and when it is happening and what, where and when it is not happening, or if there have been any changes.

Brainstorm what might be possible causes and check that they explain the differences in what, where and when the symptoms are occurring. Identify a probable cause, test your hypothesis and verify you have identified the true cause.

DECISION MAKING

What is decision making?

It is a conscious mental process that we use to choose the best option for a given situation. The decision becomes apparent to others when we take an action based on the choice we make. When people make decisions they generally choose from one of eight processes, explained below, depending on the situation, or even a combination of these. When they make poor decisions it is often for the following reasons:

They have used the wrong process for the situation.
They have used the right process but incorrectly.
They are using wrong or inadequate information.

Decision making is the area where the greatest distinction between an expert and a novice is noticed. Experienced pilots tend to have a large database of prior decisions to access, which is almost impossible to transfer to someone else verbally. Also experts know which decision making process to use, the importance of getting correct and adequate information before making the decision and where to get it; and finally how to use the time available. Although not part of the decision making process, decisions can also appear to be wrong if they have not been implemented properly.

LMQ have identified eight processes that people use in various situations to actually make that choice.

Pattern-matching or experience

This is probably the most common decision-making process, and the one used by most people most of the time when making decisions. Here we make decisions based on the pattern we see in front of us, particularly if it is changing constantly. We then compare the pattern with something similar in our mental database and choose a suitable option. An example of pattern-matching decisions are those of chess players who are faced with a familiar positioning of the pieces and can immediately 'see' their next move. Football players and racing drivers also react to the changing world in front of them and make decisions accordingly. In a social situation people can sense that things are going amiss and that an argument may be brewing. It is the pattern of body language, tone and choice of words that the participants may be using that gives this picture. We then tend to play out in our minds what is likely to happen and amend our decision accordingly. If it looks right then we go ahead and take action.

Pattern-matching is best used when things are changing rapidly or time is short. It can only be trained through experience, as people need to collect a database of patterns that they can refer to. This can be accelerated if people experience different scenarios and conditions during training. Repeating the same identical exercise over and over again is useful for developing dexterity, but not for the pattern-matching process of decision making.

Repeat

This is an easy one – just do what you did last time. It has many uses and benefits. First, it saves time and energy; second, it gives consistency; and third, it can be implemented confidently. Basically, 'if it ain't broke, don't fix it.' However, there is a golden rule on the use of this process: it should only be used if there is no new significant information.

Lottery

Another easy one – flick a coin, put names in a hat, or draw straws. It is also quick, saves energy and best of all the decision can be blamed on the super-natural. It should only be used when all the options are equal.

Pros and cons

List the benefits or the good things that are likely to happen by choosing a particular option on one side of a piece of paper, and list the drawbacks or implications on the other. Further detail can be added by prioritising each of the benefits and drawbacks, and also by assessing probabilities. Then look at the balance of the two lists and make a decision. This process is most useful for two-option situations, such as 'should I go or stop?' When there are multiple options it becomes unmanageable and less effective.

Satisficing (Simon, 1957 as cited in Klein)

The process is one where you take the first option that satisfies the most essential criteria. For instance, if you are late at night, it is raining and there is a shortage of taxis, just take the first one that comes along even if it is a people-carrier and you know it will cost more. Or, when that day arrives, just land at the nearest suitable airport.

UPS 747

On 3 September 2010, a Boeing 747-44AF departed Dubai International Airport (DXB) on a scheduled international cargo flight to Cologne. Twenty two minutes into the flight, at approximately 32,000 feet, the crew advised Bahrain Area East Air Traffic Control that there was an indication of an on-board fire on the Forward main Deck and declared an emergency. Bahrain Air Traffic Control advised that Doha International Airport was 'at your ten o'clock and one hundred miles, is that close enough?', the Captain elected to return to Dubai and obtained clearance for the turn back and descent.

A cargo on the main cargo deck had ignited at some point after departure. Less than three minutes after the first warning to the crew, the fire resulted in severe damage to flight control systems and caused the upper deck and cockpit to fill with continuous smoke.

The crew then advised Bahrain that the cockpit was 'full of smoke' and that they 'could not see the radios', at around the same time the crew experienced pitch control anomalies during the turn back and descent to ten thousand feet.

The wreckage from the UPS 747 Freighter that could easily have hit the main Dubai skyscrapers.

The smoke did not abate during the emergency impairing the ability of the crew to safely operate the aircraft for the duration of the flight back to DXB.

On the descent to ten thousand feet the captain's supplemental oxygen supply abruptly ceased to function without any audible or visual warning to the crew five minutes and thirty seconds after the first audible warning. This resulted in the Captain leaving his position. The Captain left his seat and did not return to his position for the duration of the flight due to incapacitation from toxic gases. The First Officer now the Pilot Flying could not view outside of the cockpit, the primary flight displays, or the audio control panel to retune to the UAE frequencies.

On the approach the aircraft overflew DXB heading East, reduced speed, entering a shallow descending right-hand turn to the south of the airport before loss of control in flight and an uncontrolled descent into terrain, nine nautical miles south west of Dubai International Airport. In the report a performance analysis based on a 3°-4° descent angle and a descent speed of 300kts, indicated that from the notification until overhead DOH could have been achieved in approximately 17 minutes, although it was inconclusive whether a successful landing could have been made in the circumstances.

Intuition

This is also a fairly common process. The decision is the one that feels right and with which you are most comfortable, even though you are not sure why. However, there is a logic behind this process, which is that a person's subconscious or intuition is a concentration of all the information and experience they have had. Furthermore, it also includes the mood and performance level of the person at that moment, which will affect both their motivation for gain and willingness to take risk. Intuition represents an enormous amount of data and can be considered very powerful, which is why many people rely on gut feeling more than anything else, even in the face of conflicting information. On the other hand, having the confidence to rely on what the inner voice is telling us is also not easy.

One problem with intuition, however, is that your feelings might be driven by the need for something inappropriate or detrimental to us in the long term. Therefore it is important to identify what is behind a particular feeling so that our decision is not incorrectly biased.

Analytical

It starts with identifying what you want from the decision, what you don't want and what resources you are able or prepared to spend. These criteria are divided into essential and desirable criteria, and the desirable criteria are then ranked in order of importance. Once the criteria have been established and ranked, then as many options as possible are generated and you can be as creative as you like. The options are then filtered out through the essential criteria and compared against the desirable criteria. The best option is the one that performs best against the more important criteria. Although this process can be very detailed and take time, it is also possible to use quickly, as long as the key questions are asked.

Another analytical process is Subjective Expected Utilisation, which in simple terms is balancing the value that you might get from a potential outcome against the probability that it will occur. In this process the optimum option might be an action that you are not prepared to risk taking.

Trial and Error

This process is used when there are no obvious options, so you will just have to try something and see what happens. This can be actually be done or you can use a virtual process such as what if we do this etc. This process is sometimes all you have, but usually requires a lot of resources to carry out successfully, such as money, fuel, height or time. The exceptional performance of Capt Al Haines and his crew in Sioux City , described earlier is a good example of this technique.

Decision making 'constants'

There are some constants that surround the subject of decision making.

Information collection

In all the processes the correct information must be used whether this is done consciously or unconsciously. Using communications, situation awareness and techniques for minimising fatigue or other physiological effects will ensure that the correct information is obtained.

Judgement

At various stages in all the decision making processes a person is making an assessment of the information they have and estimating the outcome. In other words, they will have to use their basic judgement of the facts in front of them. It is not unusual for people of equal intellect and experience, using the same decision making process, to come to opposite conclusions. It is why we can never know who will win the 3:30pm race at Ascot, or who will be elected, or what the stock market will do next week.

Risk

Similarly people with the same information, decision making process and even judgement can often have a different attitude towards risk. In other words, I might agree with my friend that 5–1 are the correct odds for the horse, but still feel the best decision would be not to invest my £10.

Overall Process

There is an overall process that LMQ have developed, which is probably more of a workload management tool rather than an actual decision making process as explained above.

Time. The first step is to determine how much time is available to make the decision and how important it is. The more time and importance, the more effort and care should be put into the decision.

Why. Asking why we are making the decision as this often highlights that we may be barking up the wrong tree and it gives a different set of options.

Plan B. It is useful to have a Plan B, which is something that works and can be used if you run out of time and have not managed to identify a better option. It relaxes the process and ensures we are not panicked into making any decision.

Information. Be clear on the result you want, then gather data, explore options, risks, outcomes, and prioritise as required.

Decide. Make the decision using one or a combination of the some of the 8 decision making processes.

Implications. Before taking action think of the implications of the decision. Now, one could argue that this should be considered in previous steps, except for a fundamental flaw that humans tend to have and that is we never consider the implications of our decisions until after we have taken them! I call this a double check step to make sure we don't end up doing something we have not fully considered.

Action. Implement the decision effectively.

Review. Check and the monitor the decision is the correct one. All decisions should be subject to continual review and of course further decision making if necessary.

Many airlines have a similar type process, which is familiar in different forms to many pilots, although there is normally a mnemonic associated with the each stage such as DODAR, GRADE or FORDEC.

D	Diagnose	**G**	Gather information	**F**	Facts
O	Options	**R**	Review information	**O**	Options
D	Decide	**A**	Analyse	**R**	Risks
A	Action	**D**	Decide	**D**	Decide
R	Review decision	**E**	Evaluate decision	**E**	Execute & **C** – Check

In practice these checklist type decision tools are not often consciously used, particularly by experts who have probably made the decision several times before in various forms. Nevertheless, they are useful in new situations, doubt or pressure to help the crew think in a structured manner, and also to explain the intuitive decision to someone less experienced after the event. These normally include an information-gathering step, then an analytical step, a decision step, an action step and then finally a review step to monitor if the decision was correct. The process is also circular in that after review you go through it again. However, on all of these the key step, that of DECIDE, is not developed into much detail and it is this step where the main decision making process or judgement takes place.

Experience

This is always going to have an influence on the way we make decisions and it is an area that is not easily understood. Experience is the sum total of everything we have seen, heard, smelled, tasted or felt, and thus it is a massive database of information. There are theories that all this information is still in our heads, somewhere, because unlike computers we do not have a delete function or the ability to reformat the brain. The problem that most of us have is trying to remember which file the information is stored in, and how we can retrieve it when needed. Nevertheless, experience assists us in strange ways, as we are able to make sound decisions with no more guidance than a feeling we have. Yet sometimes as our memories fail we wonder if it is all being wasted.

Group decision making

It is often easier to make decisions on your own rather than having to agree with someone else, but joint decision making is a skill that crews must develop. One of the essential things for groups to agree on first is which process they should use. Often the cause of conflict in group decision making is that the participants are using different processes. Another key factor in group decision making is the validity of assumptions. Many disagreements between people occur because the assumptions they are working from are different and they do not realise this is happening. Once the argument is in full swing and the interpersonal conflict has overtaken any rational thought, it is often too late to get any agreement. It is therefore essential when trying to make group decisions that the participants also agree on the validity of their assumptions. These assumptions are generally based on facts that can be verified, or judgements that the participants can more easily agree. The final factor in group decision making is differing attitudes to risk. Even though all parties agree on the assumptions supporting each option, they may be less or more willing to take risks.

The decision making performance indicators

Crew members use and agree an appropriate and timely decision making process

One of the most difficult things to do is for two or more people to agree on a decision. Initially agreeing the process you will use makes agreeing the decision much easier. Why people often have conflict in making joint decisions with the same information is because they are using different processes.

They agree essential and desirable criteria and prioritise

If you are using the full analytical process, described above, then it is much easier to agree the criteria and their order of importance first, rather than trying to agree the best option. The most common example of this is to agree which is the most important: the safety of the aircraft or landing at an airfield that has maintenance facilities.

They consider as many options as practicable

Within reason, consider as many options as you can. If you have the time, exploring alternatives normally bears fruit. Taking the first option that you see is only applicable in certain situations. Normally, there are better options available if you seek further information.

They make decisions when they need to, review and change if required

Notwithstanding the above, when you need to make a decision then you need to make a decision. Conversely, do not make decisions until you need to because the validity of information deteriorates over time, so it is important to be using up-to-date information. However, if the team around you requires a decision, then this becomes a 'need to'. Always review your decision and be prepared to change it if it is not working, or if you have received new and significant information.

Riyadh

On the 19th August 1980 while climbing to FL350, visual and aural warnings indicated smoke in the aft cargo compartment, and the crew decided to return Riyadh. About 2 minutes later smoke was seen in the aft of the cabin, and passengers were panicking. On final approach the No.2 engine was shut down, and the captain told the cabin crew not to evacuate. The crew continued to a taxiway and told the tower that they were going to shut the engines down and evacuate, but as no evacuation had been initiated rescue personnel tried to enter the burning cabin, but no one was able to survive. From the report:

Factors contributing to the fatal results of this accident were:

- The failure of the captain to prepare the cabin crew for immediate evacuation upon landing and his failure in not making a maximum stop landing on the runway, with immediate evacuation.
- The failure of the captain to properly utilise his flight crew throughout the emergency.

CASE STUDY

The burnt out hull of the Saudia Tristar, showing no signs of evacuation

They consider risks but do not take unnecessary risks

Flying is a risky business and getting airborne is a risk. There may be a time in an emergency when you need to take a risk because it is the best alternative; but in the normal course of events, don't take unnecessary risks. You might be able to stop in time if you are fast on a wet runway, but then again you might not. The most recent example of this and other decision making performance indicators is the United Airways A320 landing in the Hudson River. Ditching is a risky activity but the captain took the risk rather than attempting to reach an airfield or dry land, and made the decision when he needed to.

Decision Making Traps

Risky shift. We tend to make more risky decisions when we are with others.

Confirmation bias. We seek information that confirms our decision rather than looking for information that tells us we may be wrong.

Loss aversion. Once we have invested time and energy in a particular course of action then we are reluctant to change our decision.

Anchoring. We tend to be influenced by information that has set a bench-mark for the parameters we are considering in the decision. So carpet sellers in the market will initially tell you the price is $3,000, and you will feel you have a bargain when you buy it for $800. Whereas, if you tell them you will only be willing to pay $250, then you might play them at their own game and agree a fair price of $500.

Familiarity. If we read in the news papers about a shark attack then we assess the risk of swimming as high when in fact it is still probably 100,000 to 1 if not more.

How are the non-technical competencies learned?

I will cover the training for all the non-technical skill areas in one section, as the processes are fairly similar. The above skills can be learned in three main contexts.

Classroom or outdoor

As a first step, it is important that pilots understand and agree the validity of the non-technical performance indicators. This is the foundation knowledge base and the starting point for improved performance. In fact with a good understanding of and commitment to these performance indicators, pilots can go a long way on their own by reflecting on their current practice and debriefing themselves when things have not gone as well as expected. Discussion, case studies, incident analysis, role-play and practical exercises can all be used to develop non-technical skills. Filming exercises and activities designed to develop these skills gives participants excellent feedback if man-aged properly, and maximises the benefits from these tools.

In all of the above it is important that the trainer is clear what perform-ance indicators are being trained and establishes clear objectives for the training based on this. Exercises can then be designed to give trainees an opportunity to practise these performance indicators and to know how they can be improved. The exercises do not have to be related to flying as long as they are challenging enough for the trainees to develop their non-technical skills. However, it is important that trainees can see the relevance to their operational context.

Simulator

Developing scenarios or LOFT exercises designed to give pilots an opportunity of practising these skills and continually raising their standards, are the most effective ways of learning in the simulator. Also being imaginative with exercises and varying the challenges are ways that crews can practice skills in conditions that are more similar to what they might experience. A dark, wet night in an unfamiliar part of the world, when you have just done a go-around due to windshear, the ILS is unserviceable, you are short of fuel, have few diversion options and your workload is now skyhigh, is not the time to discover that you need to develop these skills. However, even on an LPC or OPC, it is important that the non-technical skills are debriefed in accordance with an acceptable methodology.

Line flying

During normal operations pilots will continually improve if constant reference is made to the performance indicators and that they debrief both when things have not gone well but also when things have gone especially well. During this debrief the crew need to clearly identify which of the performance indicators were missing or existing, and the implications of each. And most importantly how they would manage the situation differently.

Debriefing

In all of the above training activities, the debrief is the most important part of the training and where most of the learning takes place. It is essential therefore that those who are doing the debrief are qualified and skilled to do so, otherwise there is a risk that negative training takes place. In this respect, there are two techniques that trainers can use. One is called instruction and is very much the traditional show and tell method, where the more knowledgeable and experienced trainer passes on their knowledge to the trainee. This technique is most effective when transferring knowledge or skills. The other technique is called facilitation, which is where the trainer helps the trainee work it out for themselves, or to develop their awareness and insight into what they are doing and the effect it is having. This method is most effective in developing existing skills or when looking for a change of attitude.

In most line or operational training situations, it is rare that trainers have to deal with a poor or unsatisfactory performance, but that doesn't mean that tremendous value cannot be gained from the training and the debrief. Moving the trainees from 'satisfactory' to 'good' and from 'good' to 'excellent' is where trainers need to focus, because in all of the aforementioned successful incidents, an exemplary level of performance was required. In other words 'good' may not have been good enough. Remember also to highlight what trainees have done well so that it reinforces good activity, which is essential for long-term retention and developing confidence.

RESILIENCE

Resilience is an excellent word for something that really summarises all that airmanship really means. In essence resilience is about protecting yourself from the threats facing you or your environment, but also being able to bounce back from adversity and recover to normal operations, or survive the unsurvivable. Both the technical and non technical competencies that are explained in this book are the key elements that will enable pilots to develop resilience.

Other Factors

∙∙∙

FATIGUE MANAGEMENT

This may be stretching the scope of this book, but I think it is good airmanship to ensure you are physically in as good a shape as you can be, and know what to do when you are tired. The demands of modern flying these days, both military and commercial, mean that it is likely that at some point you may experience fatigue.

Fatigue is a complex subject, made more so by the inconsistent effect it has on different people. It is normally considered a long-term effect and the culmination of a long period of tiring activity. We can be mentally, emotionally or physically tired and this can be caused by a long period without rest, or as a result of shorter periods over a long time. In other words, we can be tired after a 20 hour duty time or we can be tired after 5 days of 12 hour duties. Mental and emotional fatigue is similar in that we can be fatigued by short periods of intense mental or emotional stimulation, or be fatigued after a long period. We can overcome tiredness with caffeine or with adrenalin in critical situations, but routine activity may become poor. However, we may not be able to react effectively with adrenalin when fatigued. The solutions to managing fatigue are sleep, rest and change.

Sleep

Research has suggested that the body's sleep function is rhythmical: it has periods of wakefulness and periods of tiredness. Furthermore, there are five stages during sleep, and these vary during each cycle of a night's sleep.

Typically the cycle of sleep is about 90 minutes long, and during this time you go through some if not all of the stages of sleep. The first two stages are light sleep, which enable the body to slow down, rest and recharge the batteries. They are the stages we use when we are napping, which gives us a boost for a few hours. These stages would normally last only about 20 minutes, which is the recommended period for napping on the flight deck because in these stages you can quickly recover to an alert state. In the first stage it is easier to wake up, but it is also easier to fall asleep.

In stages three and four, the body begins to enter deep sleep and this is where heavy maintenance takes place, where the body and mind are over-hauled and problems fixed. In these stages it is very difficult to be woken up, but if you are, then you tend to be disoriented and confused. These stages last for about an hour.

Finally, there is the fifth stage which is called REM (Rapid Eye Movement) sleep. This is a period of intense brain activity, when most dreams take place, and lasts for about 10 to 15 minutes. It is almost akin to the rapid alignment process in an IRU.

During an average 8 hour night there will be five sleep cycles. It is impor-tant that you complete a full cycle, but it is not a problem if you don't have an uninterrupted night's sleep. Completing three full cycles is normally suffi-cient for most people, so don't be concerned if you wake up in the night and can't get back to sleep – just wait for the next cycle and you will drift off again. Although you have missed a cycle, if you are at rest or reading a book, you haven't added to the problem. Captain Gunnar Fahlgren has a superb way of describing this: he calls it the 'sleep car' as in a railway carriage. If you miss one, don't worry – there will be another one along in 90 minutes.

Fly Dubai – Fatigue

On 19 March 2016 a Boeing 737-800 from Dubai executing a manual night approach in IMC at Rostov-on-Don but the crew elected to go-around due to windshear. After almost 2 hours holding and past midnight the crew started their second approach but went around again from 700ft. However, at a height of about 3500ft this turned into a steep descent and the aircraft hit the runway about 120 m from the threshold, killing all the crew and passengers.

CASE STUDY

So what do we do to manage fatigue? Firstly, understand what happens and how the body naturally repairs itself. Secondly, if you are tired, take the opportunity to sleep whenever you can. 15–20 minute naps are useful and getting a full 90 minute cycle is better yet, but expect that it might be difficult to sleep if you are at the wrong point of the cycle. Know your personal sleep cycle and plan accordingly. Finally, try to avoid doing critical things when you are either tired or at the wrong point in your cycle, although if this is unavoidable, it is important that the whole crew raise their level of alertness, communicate clearly, cross check and double check everything, listen carefully and monitor intensely.

CASE STUDY

Little Rock

On the 1st June 1999 an American Airlines MD82 took off from Dallas/Fort Worth for Little Rock, Arkansas, 2 hours behind schedule. In flight the crew received an ACARS message about the weather around Little Rock and suggested that they expedite the arrival to beat the thunderstorms if possible. The flight crew could see Little Rock and the airport area at 23:26 and were cleared to descend to 10,000ft. They were advised that a thunderstorm located northwest of the airport was moving through the area and that the wind was 280° at 28kt gusting to 44kt. The crew discussed the crosswind limitations and determined it was 20kt on a wet runway, and then requested runway 4R so that there would be a headwind, rather than a tailwind, during landing. At 23:40, the controller instructed the flight crew to fly a heading of 250° for vectors to the runway 4R ILS final approach course. After reaching the assigned heading, the aircraft was turned away from the airport and clear of the thunderstorm that had previously been reported by the controller. At 23:42 the controller told the flight crew that the second part of the thunderstorm was apparently moving through the area and that the winds were 340° at 16kt gusting to 34kt. The controller then cleared the flight for a visual approach to runway 4R and indicated 'if you lose it, need some help, let me know please.'

FO	You're comin' in. There's the airport.
CA	uh, I lost it.
FO	See it's right there.
CA	I still don't see it ... just vector me. I don't know.

At 23:44 the controller cleared them to land and indicated that the winds were 330° at 21kt.

CA   See we're losing it. I don't think we can maintain visual.

The first officer informed the controller that visual contact with the airport had been lost because of a cloud between the airplane and the airport. The controller then cleared the airplane to fly a heading of 220° for radar vectors for the ILS approach to runway 4R and directed the flight to descend to and maintain 2,300ft. The controller again cleared flight 1420 to land and indicated that the wind was 350° at 30kt gusting to 45kt.

CA   3,000 RVR. We can't land on that.

FO   The RVR for 4R was 2,400ft.

CA   Okay, fine.

The controller issued a second windshear alert for the airport, reporting that the centerfield wind was 350° at 32kt gusting to 45kt, the north boundary wind was 310° at 29kt, and the northeast boundary wind was 320° at 32kt, and that the runway 4R RVR was now 1,600ft.

CA   This is a can of worms.

FO   There's the runway off to your right, got it?

CA   No.

FO   I got the runway in sight. You're right on course. Stay where you're at.

CA   I got it. I got it.

From about 400ft above field level the airplane drifted to the right.

FO   We're way off.

CA   I can't see it.

FO   Got it?

CA   Yeah I got it.

At 23:50 there was a 'sink rate' warning and the airplane touched down on the runway, but the flight spoilers did not deploy symmetrically at touchdown and over several seconds both thrust reversers were deployed and then unlocked. About the time that the brakes were applied, the thrust reversers were deployed again. After departing the end of the runway, the airplane struck several obstructions.

Probable cause: The flight crew's failure to discontinue the approach when severe thunderstorms and their associated hazards to flight operations had moved into the airport area and the flight crew's failure to ensure that the spoilers had extended after touchdown. Contributing to the accident were the flight crew's:

- Impaired performance resulting from fatigue and the situational stress associated with the intent to land under the circumstances.
- Continuation of the approach to a landing when the company's maximum crosswind component was exceeded.
- Use of reverse thrust greater than 1.3 engine pressure ratio after landing.

The MD82 after overrunning the runway at Little Rock

STRESS MANAGEMENT

Like fatigue management this may be stretching the scope of the book but I think it is good airmanship to make sure you are in mentally good shape as well.

What is stress? Stress is applied pressure and a stressor is that which applies the pressure. The pressure can be either physical – environment, weight, being awake, illness, or it can be mental – and this can be subdivided into cognitive, emotional or imaginative.

Cognitive pressure is where you have too much information, more tasks than time, or are confused. Emotional pressure is where you suffer strong feelings induced by an event or a person. Imaginative pressure is where you develop thoughts of disaster. These things above are what cause stress in people and it will be different for everyone. For me I am often in dilemma. I know that one of the things that causes me stress is being bored or wasting time – having nothing to do. So standing in queues, hanging around airports, waiting for trains or for people turning up late for meetings are all bad things. Therefore I compensate by leaving things to the last moment, which means I get even more stressed when I think I am going to be late, miss my flight, and so on.

I also get stressed when I see a used drink container being thrown out of a car window, but I can quickly relieve the stress by hurling abuse at the culprit. This starts an argument and it all gets very stressful again. Life can be really complicated! Stress is greater when you are surprised by the unexpected, and/or do not have the ability to deal with it. A weightlifter with a low weight will find it pleasant exercise; a retired person with an easy crossword and plenty of time will likewise be relaxed; and during an exam when you know how to answer the question, it is an enjoyable experience. But too much weight, too little time to finish the crossword and not knowing the answers in an exam all make us stressed.

So what can we do to manage this better?

First, identify what personally irritates you or causes you stress; but you need to be brutally honest with yourself and include all the little things as well, because they have a tendency to all mount up at the wrong time. You will find that these can be divided into things about yourself and your environment or situation, and into things that others do.

Possible examples

Environment/self	Other people	Situations
• Being bored. • Running out of time. • Being hot or cold. • Being wet. • Too much noise. • A full bladder.	• Being late. • Smelling of garlic. • Using mobile phones loudly. • Not listening. • Lying. • Wearing earrings in their lips! • Poor relationships.	• Divorce. • Change of job. • Moving house. • Bereavement. • Financial. • Trauma.

Second, think about why these things cause you to feel stressed and be clear on what it is. This often gets rid of some of the items as they no longer appear rational.

Third, try to avoid the things that cause you to feel stressed if you can.

Fourth, manage these things better so that if you are subjected to them the effect is not too debilitating. If they are about yourself and the environment, then think of ways of making sure you aren't affected by them. So, I now tend to take more care over wearing the right clothing, I give myself more time, and make sure I have something interesting to read if I am caught with nothing to do. If they are about other people, then learn to be more tolerant. We all get it wrong occasionally, and so recognise that people have a right to make mistakes, be unaware or unskilled. Everyone is entitled to their opinion even if it is different from yours, and we also all have a right to do things that are important to us. Therefore, try to remember these things when the garage has said your car is going to be ready at 4 o'clock but it's not.

Fifth, do the breathing and other exercises that are recommended to reduce the physical effects of stress.

Finally, if all the above fails, let your team know what state you're in so that they are not caught out believing you are focused and concentrating on the job in hand. Don't assume they are equally stressed by the situation because they may not be – and actually could probably deal with it more effectively.

HAZARDOUS ATTITUDES

Some of the hindrances to good airmanship can be found among the several hazardous attitudes by which we allow ourselves to be influenced. I mention them separately here because they don't seem to fit neatly into the subjects above, yet they are omnipresent and waiting to pounce on us at an unsuspecting moment. I suppose the easiest way to describe hazardous attitudes is as faults in the brain's software that appear, do damage and then just as quickly disappear. I am not sure where they come from, although some expert will no doubt say it is to do with a combination of diet, genes, upbringing, or star sign. I am sure we have all done things that are irrational, pointless and stupid, and normally followed by, 'What was I thinking?' When this occurs in aviation the consequences are far more serious. The hazardous attitudes are as follows:

Anti-authority

This attitude is based on an almost automatic belief that rules and regulations are there to be broken, and that those in authority do not live in the real world. It has been the cause of many accidents, particularly in general aviation:

The unnecessarily low speed limits on some roads are just designed to catch us out and make more money for the government. And as for the SOPs that the training department produce from their ivory tower – forget it. If they did a bit more flying they would know what it is like to be a real operator. Rules are for the obedience of fools and the guidance of wise men, is the smartest thing that anyone has ever said.

Even if I reluctantly agreed to follow the recommended procedure, on my next flight the conditions of course would be different and therefore an instant amendment to the SOP would be in order. This change would be surprisingly similar to what I had always thought we should do in the first place.

Of course I could express my opinion and suggest the changes that should be made, but it just isn't worth it and the management are too stupid to understand anyway.

Complacency and laziness

This attitude is bred from doing the same things over and over again. There is little motivation to check things, plan thoroughly or maintain situation awareness, as the rewards for doing so aren't there:

Why check, nothing ever goes wrong, and I couldn't be bothered anyway. The switches are all in an eye-pleasing position so let's not waste time with the checklist. It hasn't rained for weeks, so there can't possibly be water in the fuel, and the drain check is just messy. The autothrottle is just great at maintaining airspeed so on the approach I can look out the window and enjoy the view.

However, this is one of the greatest challenges as design improves and we have such great reliability. Most pilots will spend their whole careers never experiencing a serious malfunction. It would be unreasonable to advocate super vigilance. When flying a 10 hour sector there need to be times when the monitoring functions are simple and the activity low. The key is to strike the right balance.

Impulsiveness

This attitude is all about getting on with things, and not wasting time. It is prevalent when something goes wrong and an easy way out is offered, because having a problem is uncomfortable. It also occurs when someone is lost and they will make what they see fit what is on the map, and convince themselves accordingly. Contradictory information is ignored or discredited:

Quick let's go, there's a short cut, I know what is wrong, I don't want to wait. Don't let a lack of knowledge get in the way of my impatience.

Resignation and giving up

This attitude occurs when it is all too much, we are tired and we prefer to fail rather than to confront what is in front of us and work out a solution. It often can be seen in long-distance running when the leaders have got just that little too far ahead. The most dangerous example of this in flying is when a captain is continuing with a risky course and the other crew feel helpless to do anything about it:

We're doomed, there is nothing we can do. It is all over. I can't manage it. Life is unfair.

Invulnerability and wishful thinking

This attitude is based on a belief that the person is lucky and that bad things only happen to other people. It is also the flaw with perpetual optimists whose mantra is, 'It will be all right on the night.' No, sorry, it won't be if you forget to take your passport to the airport. There is a marvellous theory that pessimists are far happier people, because they are rarely disappointed. Whereas things never go as expected for optimists, who are thus extremely miserable, especially as they have not considered any contingency plan:

It won't happen to me, I am never going to get an engine failure over water. The weather will be fine when we get there. The fog will have burnt off by mid morning, so if we just pop above cloud we will have a nice gap by the time we get to the other end. I only expected this stratus to be a few thousand feet thick, and now look – the OAT is minus 5 and we are icing up.

Graham Hill

On the 29th November 1975 a Piper Aztec flown by the racing driver Graham Hill flying from France made an approach to Elstree Aerodrome, which was in fog. Although the aircraft was well equipped and the pilot was familiar with the approach, it crashed into trees on Arkley golf course a few miles short of the runway. Another pilot on the same night made the decision to divert to Southend and landed safely. The accident occurred as the

Graham Hill's aircraft at Arkley

CASE STUDY

pilot was attempting a visual contact approach at night into Elstree aerodrome with a reported visibility of 800m. After radar advisory service had positioned the aircraft 4nm east of the runway with further descent at the pilot's discretion, he was heard to call Elstree tower and give his position as finals. The accident was caused by the pilot attempting to land in conditions of low visibility at an airfield not equipped with appropriate precision landing aids. The conditions were substantially less than that permitted by his licence, as he did not have a valid IMC rating.

Machismo and superiority

This attitude starts at a young age – 'Look mum no hands' – and probably continues until we die. There are some elderly people who are convinced they can still drive a car safely, but can't. It comes from the need to prove we are better than others, a by-product of the competitive age we live in. We are still the same person wherever we are, so it can be difficult for a pilot to play a hard squash match on one day, and then not be a little tempted to continue a poor weather approach when the competitor aircraft in front has just landed:

Only I can do this – just look and learn, sunshine. Some people have no idea, they lead such boring lives. What is the point of living if you don't have a bit of a challenge.

I think it is also called showing off, and it has been the cause of many military and general aviation accidents, as well as the odd commercial mishap.

CASE STUDY

Habsheim

On the 26th June 1988 an Air France Airbus A320 planned to carry out an airshow consisting of a couple of flypasts at 100ft. However the aircraft descended to 35ft and at minimum flyable speed. The crew may have relied too much on fly-by-wire controls and underestimated the engine acceleration time from idle to TOGA power, plus the aerodynamics of the left part of the drag curve. They went below the agreed height of 100ft AGL and during the attempted go-around, the engine, despite working perfectly as designed, did not deliver the excess thrust required to climb

The Airbus at Habsheim just entering the trees where it subsequently caught fire

over the trees ahead. Furthermore they had disabled the alpha floor AoA thrust protection, which would have provided TOGA automatically when the AoA was approaching a critical value. The Accident Commission believed that the accident resulted from the combination of the following conditions:

- Very low flyover height, lower than surrounding obstacles.
- Speed very slow and reducing to reach maximum possible angle of attack.
- Engine speed at flight idle.
- Late application of go-around power. This combination led to impact of the aircraft with the trees. The Commission believed that if the descent below 100ft was not deliberate, it might have resulted from failure to take proper account of the visual and aural information intended to give the height of the aircraft.

Curiosity

This attitude is one of a paradox. Most pilots have a great interest, if not a strong passion, in aircraft and anything to do with aviation. They are also expected to delve into technical manuals at regular intervals and learn lots of things about the subject, some of which might be quite useless. So it is not surprising that sometimes curiosity gets the better of them. However, experimenting with the aircraft is still a dangerous pastime.

I wonder what would happen if we close an engine, what is it like in a thunderstorm, I would love to experience a lightning strike. Let's do an engine-out landing for real.

Pinnacle CRJ

On the 14th October 2004 a Pinnacle Airlines CRJ departed Little Rock to reposition to Minneapolis. After several unauthorised manoeuvres the crew attempted to fly at 41,000ft, but allowed the speed to decay. The stick shaker and stick pusher activated several times before the aeroplane entered an aerodynamic stall. Almost simultaneously, both engines shut down. The air-driven generator was automatically deployed and supplied the back-up alternating current power to the aeroplane. The flight crew asked for a lower altitude and declared an emergency in order to relight the engines, but unfortunately both engines had suffered core lock and could not be restarted. At about 22:13 the flight crew stated that they had the runway in sight, but they did not make it to the airport and the CRJ crashed and broke up in a residential area about 2 miles from the airport. The National Transportation Safety Board determined that the probable causes of this accident were:

- The pilots' unprofessional behaviour, deviation from standard operating procedures, and poor airmanship, which resulted in an in-flight emergency from which they were unable to recover, in part because of the pilots' inadequate training.

- The pilots' failure to prepare for an emergency landing in a timely manner, including communicating with air traffic controllers immediately after the emergency about the loss of both engines and the availability of landing sites.

- The pilots' failure to achieve and maintain the target airspeed in the double engine failure checklist, which caused the engine cores to stop rotating and resulted in the core lock engine condition.

Pressonitis

This attitude is based on the psychological theory that people are more averse to making a loss than missing out on a gain. Hence gamblers will keep betting to recover the losses they have made. In flight, if we have managed to cover 90 per cent of the journey through poor weather, and are almost home, we are extremely reluctant to turn back when the weather finally goes below limits, and will push on regardless:

My car is at the airport, I have to get back for a dinner party. I am sure the weather will be a bit better. I just need to get through this little bit of low cloud and I am home and dry. I really don't want the problems of diverting and inconveniencing all the passengers.

Boeing 747 about to land at Kai Tak – Time to go-around? (Colin Parker)

CULTURE

I sometimes believe that the whole issue of culture is overplayed, even to the extent that at its worst it is a veil for racism, or used as an excuse for not reaching a required standard. I think everyone in the world is generally much the same and the perceived behaviour they stereotypically display is as a result of conditioning and habit rather than an innate characteristic. Often these differences are observed through particular body language, which is the veneer of the conditioning rather than a deep-rooted part of their genetics. Or they have become used to a set of unwritten rules that have been developed over a long period of time.

There are two things that stem from this belief. The first is that folk from different countries who have been subjected to the same conditioning will behave in similar ways, and the second is that any conditioning can be trained out relatively easily. People are willing and able to change their behaviour, if they understand the cause of their current conduct and the effects that their behaviour has on others, and also if they believe an alternative behaviour is more appropriate.

An example is the classic problem of not speaking up when required. I have met Australian pilots (who are supposedly not the least bit shy of expressing their opinions) from military backgrounds or oppressive commercial organisations, who when working with someone more senior would rather eat one of their own arms than say something that might be taken as criticism. Conversely, I have worked with many Chinese crewmen who were more than happy to let me know if they were concerned, and did it well – respectfully, clearly and timely. Of course this theory may be completely undermined because, with me, they had plenty of practice!

Here is a personal experience. We were approaching a remote landing site at night to pick up a casualty when we suffered a primary hydraulics failure, which in helicopters tends to make the controls a little firmer and more jerky. Through the drills, then onto the decision making, whereby my thinking was to continue to land because we had another working system. Although if this second system failed the controls became extremely firm, a little narrow-minded and very stubborn. My crewman, Sergeant West Wu (now an experienced and accomplished pilot), would have none of this – I think the thought of Edwards trying to land with restricted control onto a small, poorly lit helipad was more than he was paid for – and he suggested we should return to the airfield, a mere 15 minutes away, and use the 7,000ft of concrete that fixed wing aircraft insist on. An eminently sensible suggestion that even I could understand, and so we set off back to base, and another aircraft picked up the casualty a little while later.

I have not yet met any group of people from around the world who have not fully understood and recognised the behaviour processes outlined in earlier chapters. Nor have I met any group who are not unanimous in the belief that assertive behaviour is the most effective way to behave. I think that where the difference lies is in the level of respect that is given to certain people as a right in some cultures. In some societies, considerable respect is given automatically to elders and those with a lot of life experience, and frankly there isn't much wrong with that.

Furthermore, I have yet to hear any pilot from a wide range of cultures who does not fundamentally agree with the non-technical performance indicators outlined earlier. Although they are aware that some of these are as yet uncommon in their cultures, they fully support the need to adopt these ideals.

One area where distinct differences do occur is in body language and here again we tend to get over excited. If you do something that would be considered an insult in a particular country, although they might be amused or possibly irritated, nobody is going to be insulted because they know you haven't a clue what you are doing. However, if a local person does the same thing then that is a different matter, because it is clear it is intentional. Nevertheless, it does help with communication and understanding if you can tune into the various traits of the culture.

Another area of difference is in social or business protocols. In the Far East, the routine is to develop a relationship and personal understanding before getting down to business; in the USA, by contrast, this might be considered time-wasting, and the first thing to do is agree the agenda. However, non-adherence to these protocols does tend to cause disapproval whether you intend to or not. So you just need to learn a few basics when you are abroad, and be more tolerant when you are receiving overseas visitors, but above all treat people with respect.

If you are flying with people from different cultures, then good airmanship is also about learning the differences in body language and protocols, and adapting accordingly.

AUTOMATION

Although this area is mainly the domain of modern glass cockpit aircraft, I think for other aviators it is fast becoming a similar problem. Automation has been introduced to reduce workload, and thus make the flight safer, or at least that was the plan. A lot of automation has also been introduced to make the flight more efficient and currently probably 95% if not more of flying is a mental rather than physical activity. However, the opposite can be true if the automation system is not trained adequately or not managed properly. This can result in altitude busts, loss of speed, exceeding limitations, heavy landings, getting lost, inadvertent entry into cloud or bad weather, and even CFIT. Therefore the limitations of the human brain will be a major factor in how automation is managed. So let us explore why this might be.

I think there are six major potential problems with automation:

Over-reliance. When things work perfectly all the time, human nature will introduce a tendency in pilots to monitor them less consciously, or invest less time and effort to cross-check their accuracy or performance with other systems. In the good old days, and thankfully even with most pilots in modern aircraft using autothrottle, airspeed on the approach is watched like a hawk. A deviation of a knot or two is instantly noticed and an appropriate correction applied.

One of the reasons why airspeed was constantly monitored was because pilots knew that if they could spot trends early then things would not get out of hand. It goes back to the basic instrument flying techniques with limited panel, nip a deviation in the bud quickly before it develops momentum and influences another dimension, which is when things start to unravel spectacularly. So the development of trend arrows on the airspeed tape is another example where automation can place the pilot one step further back in the process. In other words, pilots can get in the habit of not monitoring the airspeed so closely, because the trend arrow alerts them to any problem.

Unfamiliarity. Most systems have been designed to maximise their capability and all too often simplicity is a casualty. Everyone I have spoken to rarely uses the full functionality of their video recorder or computer software, because it is either too much too learn, or when we have learned how to use it, we lose the ability through lack of use. In aircraft this becomes a problem when we get on the wrong page of the FMS and don't understand what is happening, and often make things worse by pushing buttons aimlessly.

A lack of understanding or familiarity of the automation was certainly a factor in both the Cali (where the captain had difficulty re-entering a deleted waypoint), and Air Blue (where the captain forget to pull the heading knob) accidents.

Imprecision consequence disparity. In other words a small error of input can have severe consequences, as seen with the Singapore Airlines incident at Auckland. Entering the wrong weight into the FMS will create serious output consequences that are difficult to avoid because the initial error is so unnoticeable. A single figure error in the MCDU will create an incorrect Vr. This will then be displayed on the PFD as a target speed giving it strong credibility that taps into the modern adapted flying technique – fly to target. This will prompt the pilot to pull back gently and without drama at the indicated rotation speed, at which point the airflow over the wings will breakdown and 100 tonnes of metal, fuel, passengers and cargo will crash at 130kt.

Halifax

On 14th October 2004 an MK Airlines Boeing 747 cargo aircraft departed Windsor Locks Bradley International Airport for a flight to Spain, with a cargo of lawn tractors. An intermediate stop was made at Halifax, where the aircraft was loaded with 53,000kg of lobster and fish. The planned take-off weight was 353,000kg. The Boeing Laptop Tool (BLT) was then used to calculate the take-off speeds and since the software was last used before the take-off from Bradley, it still contained those figures. The airport information and weather was changed to Halifax, but somehow the takeoff weight was

CASE STUDY

The MK Airlines B747 Cargo plane

not changed and remained showing 240,000kg. Take-off performance data were generated, resulting in incorrect V speeds and thrust setting being written on the take-off data card. It is most likely that the crew did not adhere to the operator's procedures for an independent check of the take-off data card, so the erroneous figures went unnoticed. During the take-off the aircraft began to rotate and the pitch attitude stabilised briefly at approximately 9° nose-up with airspeed at 144kt. With approximately 600ft of runway remaining, the thrust levers were advanced to 92 per cent and the EPRs increased to 1.60. The aircraft became airborne approximately 670ft beyond the paved surface and flew a distance of 325ft. The lower aft fuselage then struck an earthen beam supporting an instrument landing system localiser antenna. The aircraft's tail separated on impact, and the rest of the aircraft continued in the air for another 1,200ft before it struck terrain and burst into flames. Findings as to causes and contributing factors:

- The Bradley take-off weight was likely used to generate the Halifax takeoff performance data, which resulted in incorrect V speeds and thrust setting.

- It is most likely that the crew did not adhere to the operator's procedures for an independent check of the take-off data card and a gross error check.

- Crew fatigue likely increased the probability of error during calculation of the take-off performance data, and degraded the flight crew's ability to detect this error.

- The crew did not recognise the inadequate take-off performance until the aircraft was beyond the point where the take-off could be safely conducted or safely abandoned.

- The company had no formal training and testing program on the BLT.

Information overload. Automation typically gives the pilot enormous amounts of information but rarely is able to prioritise the key bits of information for a given situation. This has the effect of adding to the pilot's workload as he or she tries to extract the relevant data; or worse providing apparently conflicting information.

Exclusion. Similar to over-reliance but in this case the system is just forgotten about. An apt descriptive phrase here is 'out of sight, out of mind'. The TAM accident in São Paulo may have been an example of this. Because the thrust levers typically do not move in flight and the reverser on the right engine was inoperative, the crew may have created a mental picture that on landing the right thrust lever was no longer in the game.

São Paulo

On the 17th July 2007 TAM Flight 3054, an Airbus A320, departed Porto Alegre at 17:16 for São Paulo. The thrust reverser of the starboard engine was deactivated before the flight. It was raining as the flight approached São Paulo, and it was cleared to land on runway 35L. The runway condition was given as wet and slippery; wind was reported from 330° at 8kt. The cockpit voice recorder transcript indicates that the spoilers did not activate after touchdown and the thrust lever of the No.2 engine was not retracted. Furthermore, this caused the No.2 engine to increase power as it was still in the Climb detent. The aircraft failed to stop and went off the runway, probably became airborne as the runway was elevated, cleared the perimeter fence and a busy highway and collided with a concrete building, with the loss of 187 lives.

CASE STUDY

Loss of flying skills. This is not just the obvious lack of manual handling opportunities but far more important. It is the loss of the cognitive ability to fly the
aircraft, or 'authority creep'. Basically if you hand over control to the autopilot
on a regular basis then you begin to abdicate responsibility more and more
until there is a feeling that you are just a passenger in the cockpit. A comment
recently given to me by a pilot in answer to the question 'What do you do?' was
'I get flown around Europe by an Airbus'. Once pilots lose their touch for putting the aircraft where they want it to be and feeling fully in control, then they
can easily get behind the aircraft when things start to go wrong.

CASE STUDY

Afriqiyah Airways Airbus A330

On 12 May 2010 at 0401 (UTC) an Airbus A330 of Afriqiyah Airways
crashed on approach to Tripoli Airport Libya whilst executing a go-around
from low altitude, with the loss of 103 passengers and crew. It had taken
off from Johannesburg the previous evening and was expecting good conditions on arrival due to ATIS information from the previous evening that
had not been updated. However early morning fog and low cloud had
developed and they had been advised of this by an another crew that had
landed earlier.

The crew were carrying out an NDB approach to runway 09, but approach
briefing and checklists were not carried out formally or rigorously, and
although the co-pilot was PF and captain the PNF, they did not seem to be
sharing the same approach strategy. The final approach was in managed
guidance mode and then changed to selected vertical guidance. The PF
selected APP NAV mode with FPV guidance and a Flight Path Angle of -0.3

degrees but this was prior to the correct position locator, which could be because he misunderstood the managed approach procedure or he could have interpreted the captain's Track FPA call as a change in strategy. As they approached MDA of 620 ft the captain called continue which was acknowledged by the PF, although he hesitated to initiate a go-around when they were below MDA. At 280ft (AGL) and after a TAWS TOO LOW TERRAIN warning, the captain called for a go-around, which was executed by the PF with TOGA applied, landing gear retracted and flaps to position 1. The aircraft initially climbed to 670ft with a 12 degrees nose up pitch, however this was then followed by nose down inputs, dual inputs from both pilots and then conflicting inputs as the captain had taken over control also with a nose down input. At a late stage both pilots reacted to a PULL UP warning but it was insufficient to prevent the aircaft crashing just short of the runway.

The report concluded with a number of probable causes:

- The limited co-ordination between the crew especially the change into vertical selected guidance mode by the PF, probably led to a lack of a common action plan.

- The lack of feedback from a previous flight where they had had an overspeed warning on a go-around did not allow them to anticipate the potential risks with managing non-precision approaches.

- The pilots' performance was likely impared by fatigue although this could not be conclusively determined.

- There may have been effects of somatogravic illusions due to the aircraft acceleration during the go-around that would give an impression of excessive nose-up attitude.

The accident therefore resulted from:

- The lack of a common action plan during the approach and a final approach continued below the MDA, without ground visual reference acquired.

- The inappropriate application of flight control inputs during a go-arouind and on the activation of TAWS warnings.

- The lack of monitoring and control of the flight path.

Managing Automation

How should we manage the threats we face from the above problems?

I think airmanship as always would dictate understanding the systems thoroughly, practicing the functions regularly, being meticulous and careful when inputting data, and having the discipline to monitor and cross-check the accuracy and performance of the automatic systems at all times. One of the most effective habits is to think ahead and know what the system will do before it does it and being constantly vigilant. Another well known expression is 'never point an aircraft in a direction that your brain has not been 5 mins before'.

For me the key maxim with automation is the following:

Automation is your servant not your master

Imagine that you have on call an extra pilot on the flight deck who flies perfectly and consistently, never gets tired, is not very bright and does exactly what you tell him to do – but has no concept of safety and no fear of crashing. This is how you should treat automation.

Therefore:

- You maintain control of the aircraft – ALWAYS.
- Ensure you thoroughly understand the system and its interfaces.
- Use the appropriate level of automation for the situation.
- Ensure both crew are fully aware of what has been programmed.
- Monitor and anticipate continuously.

The Process for managing automation

- Decide on the flight path you want and the condition of your aircraft – your route, height, heading, speed, system condition.
- Instruct the automation to do it.
- Observe what the automation tells you it is going to do.
- Check that it is doing it.
- Monitor progress.
- Be prepared for what it is going to do next.
- Confirm that the a/c follows the flight path and is in the condition that you want.

MONITORING

Monitoring is becoming an absolute essential skill with the increasing technological developments and use of automation. The fundamental value in monitoring is that any pilot, no matter how experienced, competent, clever, skilled or disciplined, will make mistakes, lose the plot, panic, freeze, be confused or behave irrationally.

CHC Super Puma Sumburgh

On 23 August 2013, an AS332 L2 Super Puma helicopter with sixteen passengers and two crew on board crashed in the sea during the approach to land at Sumburgh Airport, four of the passengers did not survive.

The commander was the Pilot Flying (PF) on the accident sector. The weather conditions were such that the final approach to Runway 09 at Sumburgh Airport was flown in cloud, requiring the approach to be made by sole reference to the helicopter's instruments. The approach was flown with the autopilot in 3-axes with Vertical Speed (V/S) mode, which required

CASE STUDY

the commander to operate the collective pitch control manually to control the helicopter's airspeed. The co-pilot was responsible for monitoring the helicopter's vertical flightpath against the published approach vertical profile and for seeking the external visual references necessary to continue with the approach and landing.

Although the approach vertical profile was maintained initially, insufficient collective pitch control input was applied by the commander to maintain the approach profile and the target approach airspeed of 80kt. This resulted in insufficient engine power being provided and the helicopter's airspeed reduced continuously during the final approach. Control of the flightpath was lost and the helicopter continued to descend below the MDA. During the latter stages of the approach the helicopter's airspeed had decreased below 35kt and a high rate of descent had developed.

The decreasing airspeed went unnoticed by the pilots until a very late stage, when the helicopter was in a critically low energy state.

How to monitor effectively

The following process is a continuing loop that should become second nature to all pilots and is very effective at ensuring you don't get caught out.

Anticipate	Think about what you are expecting to see, hear or feel.
Look or Listen	And I mean really look and listen. There are hundreds of examples over the years where people have said three greens and there weren't.
Understand	Interpret accurately what you are seeing or hearing.
Confirm your expectation	Is it doing what you are expecting?
Double Check	Or even triple check. Often when we look at something once, or even twice we don't notice something important.
Communicate Deviations	If what you see or hear is not what you are expecting, then communicate the fact to others and take appropriate action.

What and when do you monitor

If you monitored everything using the above process throughout the flight you will become fatigued and thus dangerous, or bored and stop doing it properly. So the trick is to focus on critical phases of the flight and to monitor the things that will kill you or cause damage and embarrassment, by really increasing concentration and vigilance for these periods. It actually makes flying more fun and interesting, as you will find that you get a certain amount of pleasure from your professional approach. So, get in the habit of switching on and engage intense monitoring at critical phases of flight.

The following accidents may well have been avoided had the crew followed the above process.

Amsterdam Boeing 737

On the 25th February 2009, Turkish Airlines Flight TK1951, a Boeing 737-800, departed from Istanbul for a flight to Amsterdam. The flight crew consisted of three pilots: a line training captain who occupied the left seat, a first officer under line training in the right seat and an additional first officer who occupied the flight deck jump seat. The first officer under line training was the pilot flying.

The aircraft was directed towards runway 18R for an ILS approach and landing. The crew performed the approach with one of the two autopilots and autothrottle engaged. Flight 1951 was vectored for a line up at approximately 6nm at an altitude of 2000ft and approached the glide slope from above. While descending through 1950ft, the radio altimeter value suddenly changed to -8ft and the aural landing gear warning sounded. Once the localizer was intercepted the crew selected, by means of the vertical speed mode of the autopilot, a descent speed of 1400ft/min to intercept the glide path. The autothrottle system entered the retard mode, and the thrust levers were moved to the idle position and remained in retard mode. The glide path was intercepted at approximately 1330ft and the aircraft was now also at the correct altitude for the approach of runway 18R. The aircraft speed had during the time the aircraft was in vertical speed mode increased to 169kt, and decreased again when the aircraft followed the glide path.

At approximately 900ft, the flaps were selected to 40 by the crew and

Turkish Airlines B737 Amsterdam (Nitin Sarin)

the speed continued to decrease. At approximately 770ft, the crew set the selected airspeed to 144kt which was the actual airspeed at the time.

The autothrottle system should have maintained the speed selected by the crew but, with the thrust levers at idle, speed continued to decay. Because the autopilot wanted to maintain the glide scope, the automatic flight system, in response, commanded increasing nose-up pitch and applied nose-up stabiliser trim. The stick shakers activated at approximately 460ft, and the flight data recorder showed that the thrust levers were immediately advanced but moved back to idle. When the thrust levers returned to idle, the autothrottle was disengaged. At that moment, the speed was approximately 110kt, the pitch angle was approximately 11° nose-up and the recorded AOA was approximately 20°. At 420ft the autopilot was disengaged by the crew and attempts were made to recover the correct flight position by pitching the aircraft. At 310ft a nose-down angle was reached of 8° beneath horizon. Almost simultaneously the thrust levers were advanced to their most forward position after which the aircraft ascended somewhat and the nose position increased. According to the last recorded data the aircraft was in a 22° nose-up and 10° left wing down position at the moment of impact.

Air Inter A320 near Strasbourg

Air Inter

On the 20th January 1992 an Air Inter Airbus A320 crashed into high ground on the approach into Strasbourg with the loss of 187 lives. The crew had turned early and were established left of track, and had set vertical speed rather than flight path angle in the autopilot, which gave them a 3,000ft/min rate of descent.

West Caribbean

On the 16th August 2005 a West Caribbean Airways MD82 from Medellin to Martinique entered a stall at FL310. Even though the stall warning sounded, the stick shaker activated and the co-pilot suggested a stall, the captain thought they had a double engine failure and the aircraft crashed with the loss of 160 lives.

The West Caribbean MD-82

CASE STUDY

CASE STUDY

THREAT AND ERROR MANAGEMENT

The Threat and Error Management (TEM) concept, which was developed at the University of Texas, has become a key process in current aircraft operations. It is an overarching principle in the ICAO regulations on human factors and training, and has become a focus for much human factors and CRM training.

In flying terms there are only 4 major dangers to an aircraft:

- Losing control
- Running out of fuel
- Hitting something
- Loss of or not attaining airspeed

CASE STUDY

Bhoja Airways Boeing 737

In 2012 a Bhoja Airways Boeing 737 on a flight from Karachi to Islamabad entered an area of thunderstorms and through a squall line on the approach, which was prohibited by the Operations Manual. The captain was surprised that the speed was 30kts high as they were on autothrottle. Although not fully configured with flaps only at 5 degrees they continued the approach with windshear warnings, autopilot disconnect and eventually a TAWS alert. There seemed to be little response to these warnings and when the co-pilot on several occasions called for a go-around, the captain did not react and the final go-around was not executed according to procedures, which resulted in the aircraft crashing short of the runaway with the loss of 127 people.

The primary causes of accident include, ineffective management of the basic flight parameters such as airspeed, altitude, descent rate attitude, as well as thrust management. The contributory factors include the

crew's decision to continue the flight through significant changing winds associated with the prevailing weather conditions and the lack of experience of the crew to the airplane's automated flight deck.

Everything else will lead to one of these overarching dangers, and if every time a pilot went flying they assessed the threats in terms of what might cause the above four things then it is likely they will be safer. In addition, I believe there are some modern threats facing current pilots, which might result in the above, and these are fatigue, startle and Taleb's Black Swans.

Fatigue

Fatigue management has already been explored earlier in the book but I think it is worth reiterating why fatigue is such a threat. When we are fatigued or suffering from the effects of extreme tiredness, it is difficult to think clearly and to perform effectively, and the most dangerous aspect of this is that we are not aware that we are below par. At the time we seem to be able to do things normally, such as walk and talk, make decisions, drive a car, or fly an aircraft, but we miss things, are clumsy and not able to handle a severe emergency effectively. There is ample evidence that shows the effects are similar to being under the influence of alcohol. The combination of busy social lives, young families, early starts, long duty days, delays and other stresses, have produced many aircrew who are suffering from the effects of fatigued and can be extremely tired on the flight deck or in the cabin. Flight Time Limitations for many organisations have become targets rather than limits, and it is only the inherent commitment and professionalism of aircrew, that keeps the operation safe. Poor weather, an unusual emergency or just omitting a key action result in the threat level rising exponentially.

STARTLE

The second threat, the startle factor has become a significant factor in recent accidents. The reason for this is that modern aircrew are used to systems reliability and actually many of the historical threats are well managed through good procedures and technology such as TCAS and EGPWS. They are also used to long periods of inactivity, so when things go wrong there is often an immediate period of time when the crew are startled and confused as to what is happening. They often don't hear things and sometimes don't see things either. Communication and situation awareness breaks down rapidly and panic can easily set in. I define startle as a temporary incapacitation caused by an unexpected event, and nobody is immune to this. It is incapacitating because we are in a state of fight, flight or freeze and not thinking clearly. It is temporary but can last until the accident, and so the critical factor is reducing the time of incapacitation so that an action isn't taken that makes things worse. It is caused when things happen that we don't expect, that are of sufficient severity to create startle, otherwise it is just surprise. Sometimes these are immediate such as a loud noise or impact, or they can be multiple events that rapidly build up and trigger startle.

There are ways that aircrew can manage startle more effectively – they will never eliminate the effect – and I divide them into activities prior to the event, in the event itself and after the event. Prior to the event, the way to reduce startle is to minimise the unexpected, and so thinking of potential problems and constantly asking 'what if' will help. When startled, the technique is similar to loss of situation awareness, so recognise it and communicate to other crew members, stop what you are doing, unless procedures demand an instant response that you would have trained for anyway, manage the physiological changes by breathing properly and then assess the situation. After the event, it is important to debrief and see if there you could have managed it better.

CASE STUDY

Buffalo Dash 8 Q400

On the 12th February 2009 a Colgan Air Bombardier Dash 8 Q400 aircraft was on approach to Buffalo in poor weather. The speed decreased during configuration changes, which the crew failed to notice, and the aircraft stalled. The pilot pulled back on the control in response to the stall warning and stick shaker and increased power. Unfortunately the aircraft quickly departed from flight and crashed with the loss of 49 lives. This reaction was contrary to any stall recovery training he received and actually seemed more similar to executing a go-around. One possible reason for this could be because that was the most likely abnormal occurrence he was expecting to have, absent any system alarm. His expectation in the poor weather would be that a go-around was likely and so his brain might have been pre-programmed for that to happen when triggered. Pilots are used to not only going around when they reach minimums and are not visual, but also if they become unstabilised or if anything untoward happens. So when the significant deviation took place, even though it was a stall warning, this might have engaged the automatic response he had, was used to and was expecting to happen. Sadly, due to the combination of pitch and power, the wing dropped before he could correct what he had done and control was lost.

The Colgan Air Dash 8 at Buffalo

Black Swans

The last threat is the Black Swan (Taleb, 2007), which are things that no one has seen before and by definition are highly improbable and unpredictable. Furthermore, they cannot not be anticipated nor trained to cope with, so when crews are faced with a Black Swan situation they have to improvise and use whatever knowledge and resources they have available to them. This is why it is important for aircrew to develop resilience, which of course is the outcome of good airmanship and the use of effective threat and error management.

CASE STUDY

Madrid

On the 20th August 2008 a Spanair MD-82 was due to takeoff from Madrid to Gran Canaria, and taxied to the runway during which time and the flaps were extended 11°. Once at the runway threshold, the aircraft was cleared for take-off but the crew informed the control tower that they had a problem and were returning to the stand. The crew had detected an overheating probe and stopped the engines. The engineer confirmed the malfunction, checked the Minimum Equipment List (MEL) and opened the electrical circuit breaker that connected the heating element. However, unknown to the crew and the engineer, this action also disabled the TOWS (Take-off Warning System). The aircraft was then cleared to dispatch and the crew started engines. The CVR indicated that the crew conducted the before engine start checklists, the normal start list, the after start checklist and the taxi checklist. On the final taxi segment the crew concluded its checks with the take-off imminent checklist. The crew began the take-off and on rotation the stick shaker activated. On three occasions the stall horn and warning operated before impact with the ground and the loss of 154 lives. During the entire take-off run until the end of the CVR recording, no noises were recorded involving the TOWS advising of an inadequate take-off configuration. During the entire period from engine start-up to the end of the FDR recording, the values for the two flap position sensors situated on the wings were 0°. Over-reliance on a system, that protects pilots if they have forgotten an action, has tragic consequences when the system fails.

Spanair MD82 at Madrid

However, I believe a lot of TEM can be considered a major part airmanship. The principles of TEM are similar to those described in this book and consist of the following:

- recognizing and avoiding threats
- detecting and trapping errors
- recovering from undesired aircraft states
- employing countermeasures to manage the above

Having good technical, operational and non-technical knowledge, skills and attitudes are the countermeasures to ensure that threats are recognized and avoided, errors are detected and trapped, and the crew can recover from undesired aircraft states, so that the aircraft is operated safely, efficiently and effectively, which is of course almost the definition of airmanship used in this book.

Nevertheless, the introduction of TEM has rejuvenated the interest in this subject, whatever it may be called, and for that reason I am a strong supporter. Also some ideas resonate differently between people and if aircrew find it easier to latch on to the principles of TEM rather than CRM or other models then that is great. The important thing is that there is a need to develop resilience and this is achieved through excellence.

But why the need for excellence?

I think serious aviation accidents are like Olympic events – they come along every few years, have a big impact and are over in a couple of minutes. Interestingly, they also tend to be forgotten about fairly quickly as well.

So our approach needs to be the same and that is we need to identify how to maximise our performance and to train thoroughly and continuously, so that we are prepared physically, mentally and emotionally to deal with the situation when it arrives.

But why bother?

The big difference between avoiding aviation accidents and the Olympics is there is almost an opposite motivation. In the Olympics all that hard work, sacrifice and mental pressure can pay off with a gold medal, glory, the inevitable book and possibly lots of cash. Where as in aviation all that hard work ends with absolutely nothing at all, in fact peace and quiet and that's the way we like it.

However, it is when things go wrong that there are more similarities. In the Olympics failure results in disappointment and regret, and in aviation it is loss of life. My analysis of many accidents over the last 40 years shows a very common and recurring story and it is this. A number of unusual, unrelated and unexpected events with a combined probability in the billions conspire to turn a normal, routine and otherwise unremarkable flight into a tragedy – and it all happens very quickly, such that good, well trained crews who may be tired, confused or startled are not able to manage the situation in time. They were good but sadly insufficiently so at that moment. Once our emotions take over or we are confused then we use up thinking capacity and we find ourselves in a difficult situation.

So what can be done about it. The good news is that we know what needs to be done and that is focusing on getting the basics right and continuously improving. The challenge however is to get everyone motivated to do it.

There is a double benefit from all of this, that is best summed up in an old aviation saying which I think was restated by the astronaut Frank Borman: 'Superior pilots are those who stay out of trouble by using their superior judgment to avoid situations which might require the use of their superior skill'.

CASE STUDY

Blackrock

On 13 March 2017, Irish Coastguard helicopter EI-ICR, a S-92 based in Dublin accepted a call to provide top cover for another rescue helicopter en route to pickup an injured crewman from a fishing vessel. The four very experienced crew departed Dublin at 23.00 with the intention of refuelling at either Sligo or Blacksod. In order to make a safe approach to the landing site they elected to input APBSS (Approach Procedure Black Sod South) a company pre-programmed route in the flight management system. After a 1.5 hr transit at 4000ft the crew commenced a descent abeam BKSDA to 2,400ft and then continued the descent making a teardrop turn over the sea to run in on the programmed route. The final descent used APP1 a mode that automatically brings the aircraft to 200ft and 80kt .

The aircraft continued on autopilot at 75kt, and even though the winch operator had identified an island and requested a right turn, followed by an emergency 'come right' command the aircraft hit the side of Blackrock, which was marked as waypoint BLKMO at 282ft.

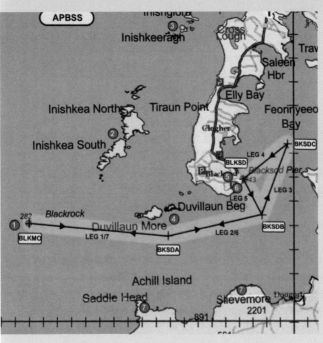

The LMQ Human Factors Model

I would like to start this chapter with an explanation of the difference between the terms 'human factors' and 'CRM', as they are often interchanged. I define human factors as:

'Anything that affects a person's performance'.

And thus it covers a wide range of subjects, such as behaviour and some thinking processes within the CRM domain, plus psychology, psychiatry, physiology, fatigue, stress, ergonomics, aviation medicine, visual and aural illusions, disorientation, distraction, noise, environment, culture, and so on.

I classify CRM as falling under the overall human factors umbrella, and consider it as a technique for managing some of these issues. The LMQ human factors model uses this basic idea as a way of understanding human performance and how we can influence it. It comprises four elements:

- Performance
- Direct Factors
- Managing Factors
- Potential Factors.

Performance

The model is headed by performance, which is a workable term for the output of a human being at work. Most of the time this performance is fairly standard; occasionally it is better than that and also occasionally it is below standard, which would include making errors. However, it is error with which we are generally most concerned, and which provides the motivation for change, so I will use error as the example for describing the remainder of the model.

The consequences arising from a particular level of performance could be considered irrelevant because other uncontrollable factors are involved. In other words, if a person drives through a red light, which is an error or below standard performance, there may or may not be an accident – depending on whether another vehicle or person happens to arrive at the same spot. The important thing to do is to identify why the error occurred and how to prevent it happening in future, without being overly influenced by the consequences.

Direct Factors

The next section of the model are the Direct Factors, which are those acts or omissions that directly and immediately affect performance. There are four Direct Factors:

Decision   The quality of the decision making.

Dexterity   The amount of physical or mental dexterity

Awareness   The level of awareness.

Distraction The amount of distraction, attention or level of concentration.

In almost every case where a person has performed below standard or made an error, it is either due to a poor decision, a lack of physical or mental dexterity, a distraction, and/or a lack of awareness (which includes forgetting). Take the example of the driver who goes through a red light, which is an 'error' level of performance. This might be because the driver:

● Has intentionally decided to go through the red light (decision).

● Pressed the accelerator instead of the brake (dexterity).

● Did not notice that the light was red (awareness).

● Knew it was red but was distracted and forgot to stop (distraction).

Another example of an error would be if an aircraft continued an approach below decision height and still in cloud. This might be because the pilot:

● Made the decision to continue because the previous aircraft had made it (decision).

● Applied power but did not pitch up (dexterity).

● Thought the decision height was 450ft rather than 550ft (awareness).

● Got a fuel warning light at decision height (distraction).

Therefore, a good starting point for investigating human error might be to identify which of these Direct Factors were directly involved in the making of the error. There may be situations where a combination of these Direct Factors is involved. For instance, a pilot may decide to continue an approach below decision height, but then lost height while busy searching for the runway lights, was momentarily distracted and hit the trees on the ridge that they were unaware were there. Conversely, sound decision making, better mental or physical dexterity, a high level of concentration and good awareness will have a direct effect on an improved level of performance.

One reason why it is important to identify which of the Direct Factors were involved in the error is that it enables the issue of blame to be better managed at an early stage. The only Direct Factor that could warrant blame to be considered, is if the error was as a result of a fully informed decision and therefore intentional. Error as a result of a lack of awareness, distraction or dexterity requires further investigation if blame is to be attributed correctly.

When professionals recognise that these are the direct causes of error, not only can they better understand how their training and the other factors fit into the equation, but they are also alerted in times of stress to be extra-vigilant and cross-check other members of their team.

Taipei ATR

On 4 February 4 2015 an ATR72 experienced a loss of control during initial climb with the loss of 43 people. The accident was the result of many contributing factors which culminated in a stall-induced loss of control. During the initial climb after takeoff, an intermittent discontinuity in engine number 2's auto feather unit (AFU) may have caused the uncommanded auto feather of engine number 2 propellers.

However, the flight crew did not perform the documented abnormal and emergency procedures to identify the failure and implement the required

corrective actions. This led the pilot flying (PF) to retard power of the operative engine number 1 and shut down it ultimately. The loss of thrust during the initial climb and inappropriate flight control inputs by the PF generated a series of stall warnings, including activation of the stick shaker and pusher.

Potential Factors

The Potential Factors are the everyday overabundance of hurdles that we all are faced with when going about our business, but which significantly affect our propensity to make errors or not perform at our best. Professor James Reason refers to these as latent errors, and the only difference I make is that I classify Potential Factors as those that are typically outside our immediate influence. These factors create the conditions for accidents to occur but they are not in themselves the causes of accidents. Many successful outcomes have been achieved in spite of the existence of these factors. We can do little about many of these factors such as the environment, but what we can do is minimise their impact. This can be done directly, or by equipping people with better Managing Factors (described below).

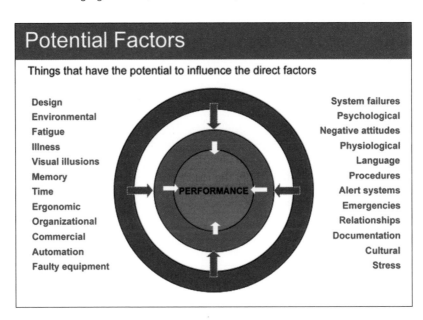

Potential Factors

Things that have the potential to influence the direct factors

Design	System failures
Environmental	Psychological
Fatigue	Negative attitudes
Illness	Physiological
Visual illusions	Language
Memory	Procedures
Time	Alert systems
Ergonomic	Emergencies
Organizational	Relationships
Commercial	Documentation
Automation	Cultural
Faulty equipment	Stress

PERFORMANCE

We can classify Potential Factors in several ways, but to keep it simple let's just put them into four areas.

Tangible external (to the crew):
Weather, technical failures, design, documentation, temperature etc.

Intangible external
Relationships, commercial pressures, financial, culture etc

Tangible internal:
Illness, fatigue, stress, drugs etc

Intangible internal:
Disorientation, fixation, visual illusions, denial, memory etc

Of the above, one of the most significant Potential Factors is the commercial pressures that aircrew face today, and the major training problem is that these cannot be replicated using the flight simulator, the main training resource.

Managing Factors

The final part of the model are the Managing Factors, which provide a buffer between the Potential Factors and the Direct Factors. These can be things that an organization can put in place to prevent error, which includes checklists, SOPs and good systems; or things that individuals have. These are the knowledge, skills and attitudes which not only can improve the Direct Factors, such as making better decisions, improving dexterity, avoiding distraction and being more aware; but which also more effectively manage the Potential Factors. It is here that CRM plays its part.

Airmanship can be considered a collective term for most of the Managing Factors that are under an individual's control and it is the training of the managing factors to a high level that develops resilience.

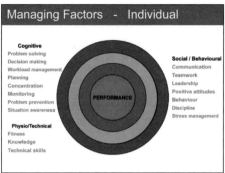

Let's look at some well known accidents to help understand the model further.

Tenerife collision

A Boeing 747 collided in fog during the take-off roll with another 747 that was still back-tracking down the runway.

Performance	Error – aircraft collided with another aircraft.
Direct Factors:	
Decision	No – the captain did not make the decision to take-off knowing that a collision might take place.
Dexterity	No – the take-off roll was well handled.
Distraction	Possibly – although the captain was concentrating on the take-off, he may have been mentally elsewhere.
Awareness	Yes – the captain was not aware that the other aircraft was on the runway.
Managing Factors missing	Communication, team-working, situation awareness, Stress management and decision making process.
Potential Factors existing	Fatigue, commercial pressures, time, relationships, language, stress, weather.

Habsheim

An A320 was making a low pass at an airshow and flew into trees at the far end of the airfield.

Performance	Error – the aircraft crashed.
Direct Factors	
Decision	No – the crew did not intend to crash.
Dexterity	Yes – they mishandled the go-around and applied power too late.
Distraction	No – they were concentrating fully on the manoeuvre.
Awareness	Possibly – they may not have been aware of how close the trees were, or how the aircraft behaved in automatic mode.
Managing Factors missing	Knowledge and skill, behaviour, SOPs, team-working.
Potential Factors existing	Negative attitudes, commercial pressure, culture, societal pressure, poor training.

Kegworth

A Boeing 737 crashed short of the runway after experiencing an engine failure and shutting down the wrong engine.

Performance	Error – power was removed and the aircraft crashed.
Direct Factors	
Decision	No – the captain did not intend to remove all the available power.
Dexterity	No – the captain did not reach for the left engine cut-off and pulled the right one instead.
Distraction	No – they were concentrating fully on the emergency.
Awareness	Yes – the flight-deck crew were not aware that the port engine had failed.
Managing Factors missing	Communication, root cause analysis, situation awareness, stress management and decision making process.
Potential Factors existing	Stress, ergonomics, design, poor training, visual illusions.

Portland

A DC-8 ran out of fuel and crashed while the crew were focused on an undercarriage problem.

Performance	Error – aircraft ran out fuel and crashed.
Direct Factors	
Decision	No – the captain did not intend to crash.
Dexterity	No – they were capable of monitoring the aircraft position while dealing with the problem.
Distraction	Yes – the captain was concentrating mainly on ensuring the cabin was prepared.
Awareness	Possibly – the flight-deck crew were aware of where they were but briefly lost awareness of the fuel state due to the distraction.
Managing Factors missing	Situation awareness, workload management, team-working.
Potential Factors existing	Design, illusion, environment, system failure.

Mount Erebus

A DC-10 flew into a mountain in Antarctica while on a sightseeing trip.

Performance	Error – the aircraft was flown into a mountain.
Direct Factors	
Decision	Possibly – the captain made a decision to descend below MSA when uncertain of position and was aware of the risks of doing so.
Dexterity	No – the aircraft was handled normally.
Distraction	No – they were concentrating fully.
Awareness	Yes – although the crew were aware they were in the vicinity of high ground, they were unaware exactly where they were.
Managing Factors missing	Situation awareness, planning, communication, safe attitudes and decision making processes.
Potential Factors existing	Visual illusions, commercial pressures, management, documentation, weather, relationships.

CASE STUDY

Polish Air Force Tu154

On the 10th April 2010 a Tupolev 154 of the Polish Air Force carrying the Polish President Lech Kaczynski crashed on approach to Smolensk Air Base in very poor visibility. Although the crew reacted to GPWS warnings it was not enough to prevent impact. The report concluded that the accident was caused by failure of the crew to monitor the approach, insufficient preparation and going below minimums. The political pressure to land plus the presence of the Polish air force commander on the flight deck contributed to the pressure on the captain to land.

Polish AF Tu 154 at Smolensk

Polish Air Force Tu154

Performance	Error – the aircraft crashed on approach
Direct Factors	
Decision	Yes – although the captain did not intend to be killed, he was well aware that there was a strong possibility that the aircraft would crash, and continued the approach.
Dexterity	Yes – the attempt to go-around was unsuccessful as they had selected the wrong mode.
Distraction	Yes – their C-in-C was in the flight deck.
Awareness	Yes – they had lost situation awareness on the approach.
Managing Factors missing	Teamwork, situation awareness, workload management, planning, communication, safe attitudes, non-compliance with SOPs and decision making processes, monitoring.
Potential Factors existing	Political pressure, organisational pressure, unfamiliar airfield, poor training, ATC instructions, late descent, documentation, weather, relationships, poor weather information.

Conclusion

Dividing the way performance is affected into these three distinct elements has the following advantages:

It highlights where resources should be prioritised and where changes need to be made. In other words, identifying if the error was more due to a breakdown in the Managing Factors or because of a Potential Factor such as poor design.

It enables the investigation of accidents and incidents to be more structured so that the network of causes is more easily understood. It moves the investigation away from blame or finding out who was at fault, and more into identifying objectively what happened and why.

It enables preventative actions to be better structured and appropriate, and avoids duplication such as unnecessary 'belt and braces' activities that can cause further problems.

If performance is to be improved then both the Managing Factors need to be improved and the threat from Potential Factors minimised. This will then translate into the Direct Factors – better decision making, improved mental and physical dexterity, better concentration and improved awareness producing a higher level of performance and ultimately less error.

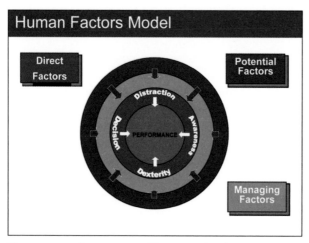

Illustrations with assistance of Jacques Lolmede

Summary

Airmanship is a combination of sound knowledge, good skills and the ability to deal with people and situations effectively. Aircrew need to know as much as they can about their aircraft and the associated subjects that will enable them to fly safely and efficiently. They need to have the skills to handle the most difficult environments and emergencies. They also need to be able to manage the task so that they make money for their companies, win the war or rescue people without wasting precious resources – but still placing the safety of the aircraft before anything else. Finally, they need the knowledge and skills to understand how human beings function, why they make errors and how to get the best out of themselves and others around them. Fundamental to this is understanding behaviour, how to manage their own behaviour and how to influence the behaviour of others.

Although I mentioned at the beginning that I have focused on the pilot because that is what I know best, I am sure that engineers, air traffic controllers, cabin crew, dispatchers and other aviation professionals will be able to adopt some of the main ideas presented in the book. Likewise there may be an emphasis on the commercial transport world, but I hope single-pilot aircraft, and helicopter folk, will be able to take some useful tips from the book also.

Epilogue

It is late autumn in the South China Sea. Pirates had been menacing shipping for some time and something had to be done to sort out the problem. It was the responsibility of the Admiralty to protect the lucrative trade routes from the East, and the Commodore had developed an effective solution, which relied heavily on deterrence as a strategy. The message he hoped to send out to the predators was, 'You are not safe on the open seas as we have a long reach.'

On the frigate the wind was howling in the rigging, waves crashed over the bow and the seamen on the afterdeck were busy lashing down some loose netting. Dark clouds had been building throughout the day and the wind had steadily increased. Dusk had long since fallen as the helicopter lifted off the pitching deck at maximum all-up weight with a heavily armed and equipped SBS team.

However, tonight was just an exercise, but because it was difficult to get ship owners to participate (the Maersk container ship was only in the area for a short while and a notice to other shipping had been posted) it had to be done then whatever the weather – it was good practice anyway. Having made sure the night vision goggles were correctly positioned and focused, the captain started drifting down to 50ft for the run in to the container ship.

Over the intercom the captain said to the experienced crewman kneeling below in the cabin doorway, 'Andy, the ship is heading 210 and the wind is southerly about 20kt, so we will approach into wind and should have enough power when we come to the hover. Even though we will be out of ground effect, we will still have translational lift and plenty of wind over the disk. What do you think?'

'I agree, although it may be a bit gusty over the superstructure,' replied the crewman. 'I can see the fast assault boats approaching the stern and the landing area looks clear. No change from the photos or the recce we did earlier.'

Turning to his co-pilot he said, 'John, I have set the rad alt warning to 30ft but could you monitor the height and your side. Anytime you don't like it, say so, and if necessary take control, get on instruments and climb to 500ft.'

'OK. They have now gone lights out.' Outside the cockpit it was pitch black, no visual references and the hazy green glow from the NVGs barely registered any detail, in the limited ambient light.

The crewman selected infra red on the nightsun and switched it on. The beam, invisible to the naked eye, allowed the crew to see the ship more clearly.

'Andy, you have control of the night sun, just keep it on the landing area. I will have to switch on the landing lights as they fast rope or else we will have a few broken ankles.'

The Wessex came in swiftly and flared over the rear stack of containers. The captain began bringing in the power as the aircraft slowed.

'Forward 20 and right, height is good,' advised the crewman.

'Torque 30, 31, 32,' called the co-pilot. The heat suddenly became unbearable.

'This is weird, I am at full power and going down,' exclaimed the captain.

'Up 5, up 10 – go-around!' called the crewman. At 500ft they considered what happened.

'The exhaust from the funnel must have given us a mega density altitude and severely reduced performance,' said the co-pilot.

'I think you're right John, and good call Andy – let's learn from that one. We will try again, running in a bit slower, and to the left of the exhaust. Brief the assault team leader – and John, can you call exercise control and tell them what the problem was.'

Wessex Helicopter on bulk carrier deck (Peter Kedward)

Bibliography

Air Accident Investigation Branch reports
National Transportation Safety Board reports

Aviation Safety Network: www.aviation-safety.net
Flight Safety Foundation: www.flightsafety.org

Brown, E. (2006) *Wings on My Sleeve*. London. Weidenfeld & Nicolson

Edwards, C. (2012) *Sometimes good is not enough*. Dubai. Airbus Training Symposium

Fahlgren, G. (2004) *Life Resource Management*. USA. Creative Book Publishers

Gandhi, M. (1927) *My Experiments with Truth*. Ahmedabad. Navajivan Trust.

Green R, Muir, H. *et al* (1991) *Human Factors for Pilots*. Aldershot. Ashgate Publishing

Hawkins, F. (1987) *Human Factors in Flight*. Aldershot. Ashgate Publishing

Helmreich, R. Klinect, J, & Wilhelm, J. (1999) *Models of threat, error, and CRM in flight operations*. Ohio State University.

Job, M. (1998) *Air Disaster*. Victoria. Aerospace Publications

Klein, G. (1998) *Sources of Power*. USA. The MIT Press

Reason, J. (1990) *Human Error*. New York. Cambridge University Press

Reason, J. (1997) *Managing the Risks of Organisational Accidents*. Aldershot. Ashgate Publishing

Taleb, N. (2007) *The Black Swan: the impact of the highly improbable*. New York. Penguin

Acknowledgements

This book would not have been possible without the input from the hundreds of pilots, helicopter crewman, engineers, cabin crew, air traffic controllers and managers that I have had the pleasure of working with and training over the last twenty years. Without their honest feedback, participation and debate, the ideas presented here would not have been developed. In addition I have been fortunate to have had many absorbing discussions with my colleagues on the CRM Advisory Panel, RAeS Human Factors Group and European Human Factors Advisory Group.

I would like to thank Lydia Malone from LMQ, with whom I have developed most of the material in the non-technical areas, and who also reviewed and edited the drafts, as well as all the consultants we have both worked with over the years, especially Sam Webb, Roger Benison and Eoin O'Doherty.

In writing this book, I would like to thank in particular the late Frank Pringle DFC of KLM and the Air Accident Investigation Branch, who meticulously corrected errors and dispensed with most of the nonsense, but also gave unwavering encouragement. Thanks also to two experienced and wise training captains, the late Jeremy Butler (ex-British Airways) and Lucio Polo (ex-Alitalia) for reviewing the drafts and making excellent suggestions, as well as Mike Varney, the founder of Evidence Based Training and Colin Budenberg of ThomsonFly for invaluable comment. I am also grateful to the late Sinisa Popovic for proof-reading the text so carefully.

I am indebted to the late Eric Brown for taking the time to review the book and write a Foreword. Eric was one of the most respected test pilots in the history of aviation, having flown 487 types of aircraft as pilot in command and holding the record for the number of deck landings – currently standing at around 2,500 and unlikely ever to be beaten. I am humbled for this book to be approved by someone with his extraordinary experience.

Finally, I must thank my wife Debby for demonstrating on a daily basis what good behaviour looks like, and for excusing me some of the household chores in order to crack on with the writing.

Index

About The Author

Carey Edwards is a former Royal Air Force helicopter pilot, who has operated in army support operations, counter terrorism and search & rescue, and currently holds an ATPL. He is a Fellow of the Royal Aeronautical Society and was Chairman of the Society's Human Factors Group, as well as Chairman of the Operations and Licensing Group for the European Human Factors Advisory Group. He has been a member of the CRM Advisory Panel since its inception, and is a CAA appointed revalidation CRM Instructor Examiner.

Carey is Managing Director of LMQ Ltd, a leading worldwide training consultancy, specialising in instructor training, human factors and crew resource management. LMQ have developed many unique materials that are used by operators, regulators and manufacturers, having worked with safety critical industries for over 30 years. Clients include many airline and helicopter operators, the military, Airbus and the UK CAA, as well as Rail companies and the NHS.

Outside of aviation, Carey has a BA (Hons) in Pschology, a BA (Hons) in Business and is a Graduate of the Wharton Business School. He is a member of the Clinical Human Factors Group and is a non-executive director of Day Lewis, Europe's largest independent pharmacy group. His career has included senior management positions in shipping, hotel development, project management, construction and manufacturing.

www.lmq.co.uk